An Analysis of the English Common Law, Principles of Equity and their Application in a Former British Colony, Cyprus

Nijhoff Law Specials

VOLUME 93

The titles published in this series are listed at *brill.com/nlsp*

An Analysis of the English Common Law, Principles of Equity and their Application in a Former British Colony, Cyprus

By

Georghios M. Pikis

BRILL
NIJHOFF

LEIDEN | BOSTON

The Library of Congress Cataloging-in-Publication Data is available online at http://catalog.loc.gov
LC record available at http://lccn.loc.gov/2016040130

Typeface for the Latin, Greek, and Cyrillic scripts: "Brill". See and download: brill.com/brill-typeface.

ISSN 0924-4549
ISBN 978-90-04-31372-9 (paperback)
ISBN 978-90-04-31373-6 (e-book)

This book is printed on acid-free paper and produced in a sustainable manner.

I must express my thanks and gratitude to my son Michael, a Gray's Inn barrister at Law, an advocate of the Cyprus Bar, for his contribution to the enrichment of this book.

I dedicate this book to the Rule of Law

Contents

England

Preface

In 1981 I wrote a book in Greek entitled in English translation "English Common Law, Principles of Equity and Their Application in Cyprus". It was a very short book, portraying in an abbreviated form the principles and parameters of the common law and equity and their introduction and application in Cyprus during British rule. As in most former British Colonies, English law remained in force after independence subject to its compatibility with the provisions of the written Constitution of the island.

The present edition, written in English, traces the lineage of the common law in a much more extensive way, analyzing as thoroughly as possible the genesis, development and application of the common law and principles of equity in England and in Cyprus, following British rule.

As a matter of practice the British introduced English law in their colonies. Its application and value is reflected in the fact that after independence most liberated colonies and dominions retained English law and became members of the British Commonwealth. This has been, to my mind, the greatest contribution to civilisation that the British offered. In many other respects British rule was unwelcome, characterized by the practice of divide and rule, which in the case of certain colonies led to their partition upon independence.

Custom and universal principles of justice were the guide to the formation, development and application of the common law. These developments, as I feel certain, will emerge from the analysis of English case law. Equity was the offspring of natural law.

Table of English Cases

Table of Cyprus Cases

PART 1

England

CHAPTER 1

Genesis of the Common Law

The English common law was evolved by the Anglo-Saxons, Teutonic peoples, who colonized England in the 5th century c.e. (common era). The migrants lived in communities in different parts of England. They shared common customs and a similar purview of the law that should govern their societies. At first no distinction was made between crime and tort. In either case the victim had to be compensated by the criminal or the tortfeasor. Either party to the dispute had a right to be heard, examined and tested by the Communal Assembly where they lived and the crime or tort was committed. This gave rise to the adversarial system of justice because either party had a right to be heard and contradict the opponent. History tells that the Common Assemblies at the beginning used some brutal means to test the truthfulness of witnesses, notably trial by ordeal.

In the process of time judicial institutions of the British communities took a definite form adopting principles of justice befitting human existence, emerging as the common law of the country. In the late 9th century King Alfred the Great, assembled the Doom book, which collected the existing laws of Kent, Wessex and Mercia, and was by far the largest Anglo-Saxon Code. For this reason in Angevin times he was heralded as the founder of English law.[1]

The conquest of England by the Normans in 1066 did not impede the progress of the common law. William the Conqueror proclaimed that he was upholding the law of his Anglo Saxon predecessors.[2] The impact of the entry of the Normans in England laid in the introduction of feudalism. It must be added that The Norman Kings, centralized the administration of Justice; firstly by establishing a King's Court by sending out royal judges to supervise the work of the old local Courts.[3]

The term "common law" was formalized during the reign of Henry II (1154–1189) of England who established the Secular English tribunals. The "common law" was the law that emerged as common throughout the realm as distinct from the various legal orders that preceded it.[4] Henry II succeeded

1 "Law Liberty and The Constitution – A Brief History of the Common Law" by Harry Potter (2015) at p. 17.

2 See "Law Liberty and The Constitution – A Brief History of the Common Law" ibid p. 35.

3 See The Rule of Law in Britain by Anthony Babington.

4 See Wikipedia (the free encyclopedia) on the Common Law.

 | DOI 10.1163/9789004313736_002

in combining all the local customary laws into a law common to the country as a whole.[5] During the reign of Henry II the first systematic treatise on the law as administered by the Royal Courts made its appearance. The treatise was known as Glanvill, produced under the chief justiciarship of Ranulf de Glanvili and is the first classical textbook on the common law.[6]

Fundamental rights of the individual were recognized by the common law in the process of its application, some of which are reflected in Magna Carta of 1215, such as freedom of movement, the inviolability of one's house and access to justice in the pursuit of one's rights. The Magna Carta declared that justice delayed is justice denied. Six months after the adortion of Magna Carta, the Pope annulled it on the ground that it was adopted by the exercise of duress on the King. Notwithstanding this intervention by the Pope Magna Carta retained its force as a guide to justice. Another significant step for the protection of human rights regarded as a follow up of Magna Carta, is the adoption of the Writ of Habeas Corpus Subjiciendum, ordinarily itemized without reference to the last word. The writ provided the means for testing the legality of the detention of a person before the Court. And if found to be contrary to law power is vested in the Court to order the release of the detainee. This was a major step for the protection of the freedom of the individual. At the same year the Fourth Lateran Council prohibited the participation of the clergy in trials by ordeal. In 1219 Henry III recognized its abolition.[7]

In 1292 we encounter the first trace of the principles of the common law in law reports (Year Books). The courts identified and gave written expression to the common law proclaiming it to be the law of the country. In some reports reference is made to the common law as the constitutional law of the state.

During the 14th and 15th centuries the Inns of Courts were established. For three hundred years they constituted one of the greatest law schools the world has ever known and may fairly be said to have contributed to the creation of the common law.[8]

From the beginning the common law was recognized as a developing system of law giving expression to its founding principles to new situations reflecting the needs of the ever evolving English society.

---

5 "Law Liberty and The Constitution – A Brief History of the Common Law", ante at p. 46.

6 See "Law Liberty and The Constitution – A Brief History of the Common Law", ante at p. 67.

7 See "Law Liberty and The Constitution – A Brief History of the Common Law", ante at p. 77, and Wikipedia on Trial by Ordeal.

8 See Baker, The Common Law Tradition at pp. 24–8, and "Law Liberty and The Constitution – A Brief History of the Common Law" ante at p. 90.

The systematization of the common law through its application by the courts and acknowledgment that it was the source of rights of the population elevated its acceptance to a high level. During the reign of William the Conqueror the ecclesiastical courts were separated from the courts of law. Be it noted that the jurisdiction of the ecclesiastical courts was not confined to purely religious matters but extended to subjects of personal status and family law. Ecclesiastical courts were abolished in 1857.

The philosophy of the English legal system is that only the people can create law through their customs and their representatives in Parliament. Professor Jaffe proclaimed that the judicial and legislative authorities are engaged in parallel in the law-making process. Of course the jurisdiction of the courts was confined to identifying and applying the common law and legislation in the resolution of disputes before them, not in lawmaking as such. Their jurisdiction extended to applying the core of common law principles to new situations.

In the 18th century Montesquieu, a great legal writer and analyst, embraced the view that the principle of separation of powers characterized the governance of England. The principle of separation of powers was first identified and pronounced by Aristotle as the balancing element in the functioning of democracy.

In the 17th century the Crown claimed to be the vestee of all power by God's grace. The courts opposed this stand proclaiming that they are the guardians of the common law emanating from the people. They pronounced that the common law and parliamentary legislation are the sole source of the law of the country. The distinguished Judge Edward Coke opposed the claim of the King in a most demonstrative way, suffering his dismissal. Coke wrote his magisterial Institutes of the Laws of England, justifying the claim that parliament and the common law were supreme in the state. The law as Coke articulated it protected the individual from tyrannical abuse.[9] The 17th century conflict about the source of law ended with the beheading of Charles I, acknowledging that the common law and parliamentary statutes were the only sources of law. The fundamental rights of the English people were reaffirmed by the Bill of Rights of 1629. In 1640 the Long Parliament abolished the Court of Star Chamber in which evidence obtained by torture was admissible.[10] The same principle was

9 See "Law Liberty and The Constitution – A Brief History of the Common Law" ante at p. 130.

10 The use of torture by the Star Chamber "was one of the important issues in the struggle between the Crown and Parliamentary common law lawyers since to the latter torture was totally repugnant to the principles for English law, as well as to reason, justice and humanity" – see "Law Liberty and The Constitution – A Brief History of the Common Law" ante at p. 109.

acknowledged in the Act of Union of England with Scotland 1707[11] (See the Rule of Law by Tom Bingham p.16). The petition of Right of 1628 is another monumental step limiting the right of the Crown to exact loans from the people without parliamentary approval.

After the revolution of 1688 and the enactment in 1689 of the second Bill of Rights it was universally accepted that the courts were the guardians of the law and legality in all spheres of life. In the 18th century the supremacy of the law was generally accepted as the only source of authority. A little earlier Thomas Fuller pronounced that however high one stands, the law is well above him. Hollsworth observed that people were inspired by unqualified obedience to the law. William Blackstone[12] proclaimed that freedom is deeply rooted in Britain. It is truly regrettable that the English did not implant the same principles in their colonies. It is worth recalling what Judge Mansfield stated in 1772 in *Somerset v. Stewart*[13] that the air of England cannot be poisoned by slavery; consequently he ordered the release of a black slave from captivity. What is distressing is that the institution of slavery was tolerated and practised in some British colonies.

The principle of attributing binding force to judicial decisions, in other words, binding precedent, was meant to convey and did convey the message that Judges were not law makers but applied the law in the way it was laid down. As the great Judge Lord Devlin observed in his book "*The Judge*"[14] the administration of justice in accordance with predefined principles is preferable to the wisdom of the Kadi, inspired as he may be.

Justice Holmes, an eminent American Judge, affirmed that the history of the common law is characterized by experience, not logic. To this, of course, one must add that the English acknowledged equity, the offspring of universal norms of justice, to remedy and complement inadequacies of the common law in its administration and application.

The word "common" signifies that the legal norms were common to the Anglo-Saxon communities. Hence the underlying principle was the acceptance of what was regarded as common to the Anglo-Saxon settlers, binding upon everyone.

The recognition and the incorporation of the common law in judicial decisions gave formal and written acknowledgment to the principles of the common law.

---

11 See the Rule of Law by Tom Bingham p. 16.

12 See William Blackstone's Commentaries on the Laws of England (1765).

13 (1772) 1 Loffit 1–19. See also Miscellany ~ at ~ Law by R.E. Megarry p. 127.

14 P. 106.

The application of the common law was not static in the sense that application of its principles was confined to situations previously resolved by reference to it. It was recognized that human society is an ever changing organism with new needs to sustain its cohesion and functionality. Therefore, the law must respond to the new needs of society by reference to its fundamental principles. The eminent American Judge Cardozo portrayed the diachronic application of the common law in a philosophical context in his book "*The Nature of the Judicial Process*". He identifies a direct dialectic relationship between the principles of law and social reality that characterizes the making of the law in much the same way as the Heracletian dialectics.

CHAPTER 2

Introduction to the Common Law and Its Application in Cyprus

Common law may be aptly described as the customary law of England. Its emergence, systematization and development is a principal subject of our study. In due course the common law and statutory law became the major sources of English law. Equity was the third branch of the English law that may be appropriately described as a complementary source of law evolved in the interests of justice.

No system of law is a priori perfect for two reasons. The needs of justice cannot be foreseen and defined with exactitude. Principles of law are as a rule evolved and developed to meet present needs of justice. The evolution of society creates new needs on the one hand and makes past solutions to their confrontation outdated. Hence the need for the adoption of principles of corrective justice to meet identified shortcomings of existing law by reference to the diachronic and fundamental commands of justice. These principles were known in ancient Greece as the pananthropic law, i.e. universal law. Aristotle defined the principles of universal justice as "εικότης" (ikotis) "Λόγος απαλλαγμένος από το ανθρώπινο πάθος", translated in English as "Reason stripped of human passion". The term was adopted by the Latins formulated as "aequitas" and therefrom by the English as "equity" – (See *Adorno's Book Negative Dialectics*[1]). Universal justice is thus identified as the corrective of human shortcomings that often derail man from the correct path of human life. Diachronically the principal role of the law was to lay down the rules of Social co-existence. Political aspirations often led to changes of the law to satisfy the interests of the rulers mostly in the field of governance. Hence we had tyrants ruling states according to their interests as well as groups who exercised power in pursuit of their commitment to philosophical conceptions as to the appropriate form of government.

Democracy as a form of government was established in Ionia identified as "isonomy", that is, equality before and under the Law. Sequentially it was adopted in Athens and other ancient Greek states, renamed as democracy, acknowledging supremacy to the will of the citizens of the city state and their decisions.

---

1 P. 311.

 | DOI 10.1163/9789004313736_003

The common law reflects, as earlier indicated, the conception of the law by Anglo-Saxon communities. The word "common" denotes universality of the principles in the English world. The law developed in response to social needs. The conquest of England by the Normans did not halt or impede the development of the common law. On the contrary, the Normans became part of the English society, contributing themselves to the evolution of the common law. The Magna Carta of 1215 can be identified as a charter of inalienable rights. It was a charter of human rights.

In this book we shall follow the development of the common law, its application by the courts and its hypostasis viewed in juxtaposition with legislative enactments.

In parallel we shall examine the roots of equity, wherefrom it sprang, and sequential progress leading to its acknowledgment as an indispensable element of justice and its administration. Equity complemented the common law, providing the stamp of corrective justice.

Common law evolved through the years in response to the needs of the English society. Equity reflects the principles of universal justice developed as a corrective of applicable law to mitigate its rigour when eternal justice so required. Statutory law complemented the framework of English law emerging from the people, be it indirectly through its representatives.

England was the greatest colonial power in the modern era. English law in a codified form and principles of the common law and equity were transplanted in English colonies and dominions including Cyprus. After the end of the colonial era principles of English Law remained in force in many former colonies and dominions, taking part in the British Commonwealth. In Cyprus, as earlier indicated, English law in its entirety was maintained after Independence, subject to the written Constitution of the country that safeguarded to a great extent human rights according to the prototype of international human rights charters and conventions. Article 188.1 of the Constitution provides that the courts will enforce existing law of the country subject to the Constitution. Hereafter we quote Article 188.1 in the interests of exactitude:

> Subject to the provisions of this Constitution and to the following provisions of this Article, all laws in force on the date of the coming into operation of this Constitution shall, until amended, whether by way of variation, addition or repeal, by any law or communal law, as the case may be, made under this Constitution, continue in force on or after that date, and shall, as from that date be construed and applied with such modification as may be necessary to bring them into conformity with this Constitution.

Article 25 of the Courts of Justice Law 14/60 enacted soon after Independence provided that the existing law at the date of Independence shall remain in force including the common law and principles of equity.

The English assumed the occupation and administration of Cyprus in 1878 following a Defence Treaty with Turkey under whose occupation Cyprus came in 1571. Sovereignty remained with Turkey. In 1914, when England and Turkey became adversaries during the First World War, England denounced the treaty of 1878 and proclaimed Cyprus to be an English colony. Thereafter, in 1925, following the Treaty of Lausanne at which Turkey disclaimed any right over Cyprus, Cyprus was declared to be a Crown colony.

When the English took over the administration of Cyprus, Ottoman Law was in force. The report of the English Consul in Cyprus of 1867, Sandwith, is characteristic of the administration of justice during Ottoman rule. He says, inter alia, that the bad administration of justice caused great damage to Cyprus, constituting a major factor to the lack of progress in the country.[2]

It must be noted that before reforms were introduced by Ottomans in 1839 under pressure from European countries – the Tanzimat – the Greeks of Cyprus, constituting the vast majority of the population, were in all respects regarded and treated as inferior subjects. Be it noted that when the Turks occupied Cyprus in 1571 there were no Turks in the island. Before the Tanzimat not only the Greeks did not participate in the administration of justice but more than that they were not accepted even as witnesses in judicial proceedings. Even after the Tanzimat there were many deficiencies in the administration of justice, as Hill notes in his book on the History of Cyprus.

In accordance with their practice, the English introduced English law in their colonies gradually. So they did in Cyprus. First they took steps to introduce humanitarian principles in the administration of justice, including the manning of the courts. Gradually they introduced principles of the English law in codes on different subjects. The process of Anglicizing the law of Cyprus was completed in 1935 by the introduction of the Courts of Justice Order making English substantive and procedural law in its totality applicable in the country. The citizens of the country experienced relief from the replacement of Ottoman law with English law.

2 Saville "Cyprus", 1878.

CHAPTER 3

Application and Development of the Common Law

The development of the common law was gradual but steady. The field of its application was unfailingly extended to meet new needs and fill gaps in its framework. It is no exaggeration to say that the common law emerged, developed and progressed in line with human needs and lessons of experience and knowledge. Hereafter reference is made to a number of judicial decisions that bear out the above.

In *R. v. Halpin*[1] the Court underlined that the principles of the law must be applied in the light of present reality. The declaration of Lord Denning in *Liverpool C.C v. Irwin*[2] is relevant in this connection: "Judges should develop the law, case by case, as they have done in the past. They must not await the Law Commission".

The commitment to the rights of a person was unabating. In *R.v. Barnsley & M.B.C.*[3] it was emphasized that the rights of a person at common law should be in compliance with natural justice. This reflects the anxiety of society that the human rights of a person should find proper recognition in the law. As Lord Diplock discerned in *de Lasala v. de Lasala*,[4] it became generally accepted that the common law is not unchanging but it develops to meet the changing circumstances and patterns of the society to which it is applied. But, as underlined in another case, judges should not under the guise of interpretation provide their preferred amendments of statutes something that would undermine the impartiality of the Judiciary.[5] One can remark that Judges can expand the law by applying the common law to new situations by reference to its core principles not by evolving legal principles of their choice. The role of Judges in the judicial process is aptly defined by Lord Diplock in *Re Racal Communications*.[6]

In *Haron v. Central Securities*[7] the Court of Appeal stressed the desirability that the development of the common law should be homogenous in the various countries of the Commonwealth.

1 (1975) 2 All E.R. 1124 (C.A.).
2 (1975) 3 All E.R. 658 (C.A.).
3 (1976) 3 All E.R. 452 (C.A.).
4 (1979) 2 All E.R. 1146 (P.C.).
5 Duport Steels Ltd. v. Sirs, (1980) 1 All E.R. 529 (H.L.).
6 (1980) 2 All E.R. 634 (H.L.).
7 (1982) 2 All E.R. 481 (P.C.).

 | DOI 10.1163/9789004313736_004

In another case, *Invercargill City Council v. Hamlin*,[8] the Privy Council dealing with the application of the common law in New Zealand acknowledged that the Court of Appeal of New Zealand was entitled to develop the common law according to local policy considerations in areas where the common law was developing, not settled.

In *Palmer v. Bowman*[9] the Court of Appeal observed in relation to an Australian decision on the common law that the decision was not binding in England recognizing that the common law may have taken different paths in opposite sides of the world.

The common law recognized fundamental constitutional rights as the European Convention on Human Rights does. Freedom of expression was one of them.[10]

In *R. (Rottman) v. Commissioner of Police*[11] it was stressed that the common law is not extinguishable by statute unless this is made clear by the statute or by clear implication. In the same case it was pointed out that the common law is applied in a manner making possible its application in modern times. Thus the power vested by the common law to search the premises of an arrestee applied to arrests made pursuant to extradition proceedings.

Below we shall refer to some other principles of the common law.

In *D. v. B.*[12] it was affirmed that at common law one's name is the name by which he is known.

The Rules of litigation evolved under the common law are inapplicable to administrative inquiries.[13]

The right to join a union safeguarded by Article 11(1) of the European Convention on Human Rights did constitute a fundamental principle of the common law.[14]

Under the common law no interest is recoverable for a late or withheld payment.[15]

When a statute covers comprehensively a subject, there is no justification to resort to the common law or equity.[16]

---

8 (1996) 1 All E.R. 756 (P.C.).

9 (2000) 1 All E.R. 22 (C.A.).

10 R. (Profile Alliance) v. B.B.L., (2002) 2 All E.R. 756 (C.A.).

11 (2002) 2 All E.R. 865 (H.L.) see also the Australian decision Bropho V State of Western Australian 1990 171 CLR1.

12 (1979) 1 All E.R. 92 (C.A.).

13 Bushell v. Secretary of State, (1980) 2 All E.R. 608 (H.L.).

14 Cheall v. APEX, (1982) 3 All E.R. 855 (C.A.).

15 Techno – Impex v. van Weelde, (1981) 2 All E.R. 689 (C.A.).

16 Sevenoaks D.C. v. Pattullo & Vinson Ltd., (1984) 1 All E.R. 544 (C.A.).

At common law there was neither a general nor a particular right to privacy.[17]

International organizations enjoyed no sovereign or diplomatic immunity under the common law. Such immunity was conferred by statute.[18]

In *R. v. Bournewood – N.H.S. Trust*[19] the Court dealt with what amounted to imprisonment at common law. Any restraint within defined bounds which is a restraint in fact may amount to imprisonment. In the particular case the House of Lords found by majority that the mental patient accommodated in an unlocked ward was not imprisoned.

Under the common law the Crown was not liable in tort. Liability was established by statute.[20]

In *Sadaway v. Bethlem Royal Hospital*[21] it was emphasized that it is undesirable to formulate a different aspect of duty with precision. This is not the way the common law develops. What must be precisely defined is the general duty of care.

Decisions cited herein below shed light on the compass and development of the common law.

In *R. v. Connor*[22] the court affirmed that the common law is by and large a judge made rule where the reasons of its existence stop this may appropriately qualify its reach. The court added: "So far as Judges have propounded a rule which, in the light of experience, is potentially productive of injustice, it is not beyond their power to put the matter right".

In *R. v. Smith (Wallace Duncan) (No. 4)*[23] reference is made with approval to the development of the common law to meet contemporary needs of society. The common law developed incrementally and logically, as stressed in *R. v. Dhaliwal.*[24]

In *R.C.C. v. Total Network*[25] it was held that for a statutory scheme to supersede the common law it has to be positively shown to be inconsistent with it. On the other hand the court should not extend the common law principles in areas where Parliament has made recent and detailed intervention.[26] But a common law rule is not abrogated by statute unless the subject matter of the

---

17 Malone v. Commissioner of Police, (1979) 2 All E.R. 620 (Megarry V-C).

18 Standard Bank v. I.T.C., (1986) 3 All E.R. 257.

19 (1998) 3 All E.R. 289 (H.L.).

20 Trawnik v. Gordon Lennox, (1985) 2 All E.R. 368 (C.A.).

21 (1985) C.A. 871.

22 (2004) 1 All E.R. 925 (H.L.).

23 (2004) 2 Cr.App.R. 269.

24 (2006) 2 Cr.App.R. 348 (24) – 2 Cr.App.R. 349 (2).

25 (2008) 2 All E.R. 413 (H.L.).

26 Birmingham v. Shafi, (2009) 3 All E.R. 127 (C.A.).

rule is the subject of specific legislative provision. The remarks of Lord Rodger in *Secretary of State v. Meier*[27] are enlightening: "And, of course, the common law does evolve by making pragmatic incremental developments. But, if they are to work, they must be consistent with basic principle and they must make sense".

At common law an open system of justice is the rule. The open justice principle aims to allow the public as well as the press to understand the justice system and scrutinize it, as underlined in Guardian v. Westminster Magistrates.[28]

In *A Local Authority v. D.L.*[29] it was stressed that the court has inherent jurisdiction at common law to protect the autonomy of the individual from interference or submission. The common law jurisdiction on the subject is compatible with Article 8 of the European Convention on Human Rights. The court propounded the position that "ability of the common law to develop and adapt its jurisdiction on a case by case basis, as might be required, would meet the need more readily".

Procedural fairness is an aspect of the common law coinciding with Article 5(4) of the European Convention on Human Rights. Principles of open justice could be developed by the courts under the common law without need arising to be adopted by a statute, as confirmed in *Kennedy v. Charity Commission.*[30]

The Common Law was adopted in former British colonies, except those that were previously colonised by other nations. Most British colonies revolted again British Rule a number of them with military means. Notwithstanding this opposition of the colonies to English Rule, following their liberation they kept English law first and foremost the common law as the law of their countries.

The retention of the English common law is no coincidence. The Common Law did not arise from any belief in superior principles or rules. It emerged from the lessons of life that gave universal dimensions and strength to human co-existence. Detailed reference to the countries which retained the common law after independence is made in the Wikipedia, the free encyclopedia. About one third of the worlds' population (approximately 2.3 billion people) live in common law jurisdictions in a few of which the system is mixed with civil law. Common law finds application in twenty four or twenty five countries, including some highly populated ones, such us India, United States of America, Pakistan, Nigeria, Canada, Bangladesh, Australia, Canada.

---

27 (2010) 1 All E.R. 855 (S.C.).

28 (2012) 3 All E.R. 551 (C.A.).

29 (2012) 3 All E.R.. 1064 (C.A.).

30 (2014) 2 All E.R. 847 (S.C.).

The genesis extension, systematization and general application of the Common law have been subjects of high estimation by distinguished jurists. Professors D. Williams and Hume in their work on Human Rights under the Australian Constitution, identified the common law as "a vibrant and rich source of human rights". Sir Edward Coke evaluated the Common law as "a perfection of reason" (C.F.A. Lawson, the Strength of English Law). American jurists stressed that the common law is the offspring of experience wherefrom principles of law emerge deductively (see reference to the analysis of the Common Law by Justice Holme and Justice Cartozo).

CHAPTER 4

Binding Precedent

In the course of time the principle of binding judicial precedent gained roots as a fundamental principle of the administration of justice.

The object of binding precedent is to ensure certainty about the law and institutionally lay down that the authority of judges is confined to the application of the law, not the making of it.

At the core of the doctrine of binding precedent lies the principle that in the hierarchy of the judiciary lower courts are bound by the principles identified and applied by higher courts. Thus the decisions of the Judicial Committee of the House of Lords and sequentially of the Supreme Court are binding on the Court of Appeal and lower courts and decisions of the Court of Appeal are binding on the High Court and the courts below. Decisions of the House of Lords and sequentially the Supreme Court are not invariably binding on the Supreme Court. Nevertheless in practice they are followed unless founded on a demonstrably wrong principle.

The principle of binding precedent, significant as it is, is designed to ensure certainty of the law. On the other hand, as Lord Diplock observed in *de Lasala v. de Lasala*,[1] "judicial decisions would not tie the law to anachronistic principles". As the learned Judge stressed "The common law is not static, leaving room to the courts to develop it to meet new social circumstances".

The principles of the common law are malleable, flexible to the extent of applying to new circumstances without changing their character or physiognomy. Else the common law in the process of time would become anachronistic.

Up until 1966 the Judicial Committee of the House of Lords regarded itself bound by previous decisions of the court. This approach was abandoned in 1966[2] by the House of Lords composed of the totality of its members on the ground that strict adherence to the principles of previous decisions may cause injustice and impose unjustified restrictions to the development of the law. Simultaneously the court underlined that binding precedent retained it status, departure from which was an exception. Deviation or departure from a previous decision can find justification only in face of objective reasons notably that the previous decision did not give expression to the applicable law.

1 (1979) 2 All E.R. 1146 (P.C.).
2 *Note*, (1966) 3 All E.R. 77.

 | DOI 10.1163/9789004313736_005

Disagreement with the result as such with a previous decision does not provide ground for departing from it.

In *Young v. Bristol Aeroplane Co. Ltd.*[3] it was decided that the Appeal Court was bound by its previous decisions subject to certain exceptions: When two or more decisions of the Court of Appeal are in conflict, the court may follow the one it regards as correct without any restrictions as to its choice.

In *Sims v. William Howard & Son Ltd.*[4] observations were made to the effect that if there were conflicting decisions on matters of practice, the most recent one should be followed.

In face of conflicting decisions of the House of Lords and the Court of Appeal, the former should be followed.

There is a right to depart from a previous decision of the Court of Appeal if it was issued per incuriam, i.e. without due regard to the principles of law in force at the time of its issuance.

The above case was affirmed on appeal.[5]

In *Davis v. Johnson*[6] the Court of Appeal, composed of 5 judges, ruled that it has the right to depart from a previous wrong decision, the wrongfulness of which is evident. The decision was affirmed by the House of Lords, reminding at the same time that the decision in *Young v. Bristol* retains its force.[7] The H.L. emphasized the need for the CA to follow precedent as a fundamental rule of the administration of Justice. The decision in the case is associated with the facts surrounding it. If any principle can be deduced it is that the CA can depart from a previous decision if demonstrably contrary to law.

On a review of the principle of binding precedent it appears with relatively minor exceptions to be dominant. The scope of departure from it is limited, underlying the principle that Judges are not law makers but the guardians of the law.

R v Gold (1968) 1 All E.R. 849 (C.A.) acknowledged greter amenity to depart from judicial president in criminal cases affecting the liberty of the subject. The relevant dicta were adopted in the subsequent decision of *R v Newsom (1970) 3 All ER 455* (see also *R v Spencer (1985) 1 ALL ER 673*).

3 (1944) 2 All E.R. 293 (C.A.).

4 (1964) 1 All E.R. 918 (C.A.).

5 (1946) 1 All E.R. 98.

6 2 (1978) 1 All E.R. 841.

7 Davis v. Johnson, (1978) 1 All E.R. 1332.

CHAPTER 5

Basic Principles of the Common Law

The basic principles of the common law aim to uphold the rights of man and ensure social cohesion. They are akin to what in modern times are identified as constitutional rights. England never had a written Constitution. One can legitimately say that the common law was a substitute for a written constitution, gradually extending to meet new social needs; so much so that England qualified as a country with a developing code of human rights. The common law recognized fundamental constitutional rights as the European Convention on Human Rights does. Freedom of expression was one of them.[1]

As Lord Denning asserted in *Liverpool C.C. v. Irwin*,[2] Judges should develop the law, case by case, as they have done in the past. They must not await the Law Commission.

As elsewhere noted, the rights of a person at common law require that there should be compliance with the rules of natural justice. Common law recognized fundamental constitutional rights. Part of the constitutional role of the courts is to interpret the law and expand the common law and equity.[3]

At common law there was neither a general nor a particular right to privacy.[4]

Time and again it was stressed that it is important that the development of the common law in parts of the world where it is applicable should be homogenous. Nonetheless it is realized that change of circumstances in Commonwealth countries may be different to changes that came about in England. Thus in *Palmer v. Bowman*[5] the Court of Appeal rejected an Australian decision on the application of the common law in Australia, saying that the decision is not binding on the court, noting that the common law may well have followed different paths in opposite sides of the world.

The common law is not extinguished by statute unless this is made clear by the statute or by clear indication. The common law is applied in a manner making its application possible in modern times.

When a code covers comprehensively a subject, there is no justification to resort to the common law or equity because they appear to achieve a fairer

1 R. (Profile Alliance) v. B.B.L., (2002) 2 All E.R. 756 (C.A.).
2 (1075) 3 All E.R. 658.
3 Re Racal Communications, (1980) 2 All E.R. 634 (H.L.).
4 Malone v. Commissioner of Police, (1979) 2 All E.R. 620 (Mcgarry V-C).
5 (2000) 1 All E.R. 22 (C.A.).

 | DOI 10.1163/9789004313736_006

result. As noted in *R. (Rottman) v. Commissioner of Police*,[6] it is undesirable to formulate different aspects of the duty of care with precision. This is not the way the common law develops. What must be precisely defined is the general duty of care. The common law develops to meet the contemporary needs of society. The court should not extend the principles of the common law to areas where Parliament has made recent and detailed intervention.

The common law recognized constitutional rights. Part of the constitutional role of the court is to interpret the law and expound the principles of the common law and equity.[7]

It has been repeatedly said that the development of the common law in the various parts of the Commonwealth should be homogenous. In *Haron v. Central Securities*[8] the court repeated what was said by Parker, L.J., in *Smith v. Leech Brown & Co. Ltd.*:[9] "It is important that the common law, and the development of the common law, should be homogenous in various sections of the Commonwealth".

Of course, it should not be forgotten that the common law by reference to its basic principles develops by application to new previously unknown circumstances. Inevitably social complexion in the various countries of the Commonwealth is not the same. In *Palmer v. Bowman*[10] the Court of Appeal refused to follow an Australian decision saying: "The decision is not binding on me and the common law may well have followed different paths in opposite sides of the world".

When an equitable remedy has its counterpart at common law, equity will by analogy to common law hold the remedy to be subject to the same period of limitation. Again if equity extends the right of action to parties who would not have a remedy at common law, the action would again be subject to the common law period of limitation.

Interference with the freedom of the press is a matter of particular importance; so it has been treated at common law.[11] Likewise the common law recognizes the right to freedom of expression as a fundamental right in the same way as the European Convention on Human Rights does.[12]

---

6 (2002) 2 All E.R. 865 (H.L.).

7 Re Racal Communications, (1980) 2 All E.R. 634 (H.L.).

8 (1982) 2 All E.R. 481 (P.C.).

9 (1966) 3 All E.R. 1159, 1162.

10 (2000) 1 All E.R. 22 (C.A.).

11 A. v. B., (2002) 2 All E.R 545 (C.A.).

12 R. (Profile Alliance) v. B.B.C., (2002) 2 All E.R. 756 (C.A.).

The common law is not extinguishable by statute unless this is made clear by the statute or by clear implication.[13] In the same decision the Judicial Committee of the House of Lords stressed that the common law is enforced in a manner making possible its application in modern conditions. Thus the power at common law to search the premises of the arrestee applied to arrests made pursuant to extradition decisions.

The principles of the common law must be applied in the light of present reality.[14] The observations of Lord Denning in *Liverpool C.C. v. Irwin*[15] that Judges should develop the common law case by case, as they have done in the past is not to be ignored. They should not await the Law Commission.

The decision in *R. v. Barnsley M.B.C.*[16] is fundamental, stressing that the rights of a person at common law should be in compliance with the rules of natural justice. It must be noted that the range of fundamental rights recognized by the common law was not as extensive as the rights recognized by modern Charters and Conventions on Human Rights. The right to privacy was not recognized as an inalienable right at common law.[17]

It may be noted that at common law one's name is the name by which he/she is known. Of great significance is the ascertainment of Lord Diplock in *de Lasala v. de Lasala*[18] that it has become generally accepted at the present day that common law is not unchanging but develops with changing circumstances and patterns of society to which it is applied. What judges must never do is to provide their preferred amendment to statutes under the guise of interpretation. Such a course would undermine the impartiality of the Judiciary.[19]

Rules of litigation evolved under the common law are inapplicable to administrative inquiries.[20]

It may be noted that the right to join a union safeguarded by Article 11(1) of the European Convention on Human Rights was recognized as a fundamental principle of the common law.[21]

---

13 R. (Rottman) v. Commissioner of Police, (2002) 2 All E.R. 865 (H.L.).
14 R. v. Halpin, (1975) 2 All E.R. 1124 (C.A.).
15 (1973) 3 All E.R. 658 (C.A.).
16 (1976) 3 All E.R. 452 (C.A.).
17 Malone v. Commissioner of Police, (1979) 2 All E.R. 620 (Megarry, V-C).
18 (1979) 2 All E.R. 1146 (P.C.).
19 Duport Steels Ltd. v. Sirs, (1980) 1 All E.R. 529 (H.L.).
20 Bushell v. Secretary of State, (1980) 2 All E.R. 608 (H.L.).
21 Cheall v. Apex, (1982) 3 All E.R. 855 (C.A.).

When a statute covers comprehensively a subject, there is no justification to resort to common law or equity on the ground that their principles appear to achieve a fairer result.[22]

Under the common law it is undesirable to formulate different aspects of the duty of care with precision. This is not the way the common law develops. What must be precisely defined is the general duty of care. Under the common law the Crown was not liable in tort.[23]

In the course of time after judicial identification of the principles of the common law and in due course the application of its principles to meet new situations it came to be known as judge made law. However, if the reason or acknowledgment of a rule ceased to be of judicial need, jurisdiction vests in the court to stop it or qualify it.[24] In the same decision it is pointed out that a rule evolved by the judges in the context of the development of the common law if in the light of experience is productive of injustice, it is not beyond the power of the court to put the matter right.

The development of the common law to meet contemporary needs of society is a matter that was often underlined by the courts.[25]

The common law develops incrementally and logically, as recognized in *R. v. Dhaliwal*.[26] For a statutory scheme to supersede the common law it has to be positively shown to be inconsistent with the common law.[27]

Also the court should not extend common law principles in areas where Parliament has made recent and detailed interventions.[28]

The common law rule is not abrogated by statute unless the subject matter of the rule is the subject of specific legislative provision.[29]

Enlightening are the observations of Lord Rodger in *Secretary of State v. Meier*:[30] "And, of course, a common law does evolve by making pragmatic incremental development. But, if they are to work, they must be consistent with basic principles and they must make sense".

At common law an open system of justice was established. The open justice principles aim to allow the public as well as the press not only to understand the justice system but also to scrutinize it.[31]

---

22 Pioneer Aggregates Ltd. v. Secretary of State, (1984) 2 All E.R. 358 (H.L.).
23 Trawnik v. Gordon Lennox, (1985) 2 All E.R. 368 (C.A.).
24 R. v. Connor, (2004) 1 All E.R. 925 (H.L.).
25 R. v. Smith (Wallace Duncan) (No. 4), (2004) 2 Cr.App.R. 269 (C.A.).
26 (2006) 2 Cr.App.R. 348 (24), 349 (2).
27 R.C.C. v. Total Network, (2008) 2 All E.R. 413 (H.L.).
28 Birmingham v. Shafi, (2009) 3 All E.R. 127 (C.A.).
29 R. (K.P.A.G.) v. The Secretary of State, (2009) 3 All E.R. 633.
30 (2010) 1 All E.R. 855 (S.C.).
31 Guardian v. Westminster Magistrates, (2012) 3 All E.R. 551 (C.A.).

The court has inherent jurisdiction at common law to protect the autonomy of the individual from interference or submission, a principle compatible with Article 8 of the European Convention on Human Rights. The ability of the common law to develop and adapt its jurisdiction on a case by case basis, as might be required, would meet arising needs of justice.[32]

Procedural fairness was a fundamental aspect of the common law likewise guaranteed by the European Convention on Human Rights. Principles of open justice, as acknowledged, could be developed by the courts as a matter of common law without need arising to be coded in a statute. The Privy Council acknowledged that the New Zealand Court of Appeal was entitled to develop the common law according to local policy considerations in areas of the common law that were developing, not settled.[33]

Lastly it may be noted that international organizations enjoyed no sovereign or diplomatic immunity under the common law. Such immunity was conferred by statute.[34]

32 A Local Authority v. D.L., (2012) 3 All E.R. 1064 (C.A.).

33 Invercargill City v. Hamlin, (1996) 1 All E.R. 756 (P.C.).

34 Standard Bank v. I.T.C. (1986) 3 All E.R. 257 (Binghar, J.).

CHAPTER 6

The Administration of Justice

Natural justice is at the root of the common law rules relevant to the administration of justice.

In *Fairmount Investments v. Secretary of State*[1] Lord Russell of Killowen affirmed that every Act incorporates the rules of natural justice. At common law, too, fair trial is a tenet of the judicial system. No conviction is safe unless the offspring of a fair trial.[2]

Both at common law and under the European Convention on Human Rights before the conclusion of the proceedings the court should know the views of the parties about the issues and the evidence before them. At common law justice has to be demonstrated in public save in the face of highly exceptional circumstances.[3]

Procedural fairness is a basic principle of the common law, a right presently guaranteed by Articles 5(4) and 6(3) of the European Convention on Human Rights.[4]

The common law duty of procedural fairness extended to the gaining of information and the reasons for its classification. The duty arose where the liberty or the status of a person was at issue. In the case cited hereafter declaratory relief was granted – *R. (Ali) v. Director of High Security.*[5]

In *R. v. Daniel*[6] it was unqualifiedly held that a litigant has an unfettered right to be represented by counsel and, as in the aforesaid case this right was denied, the decision of the trial court was annulled.

Criminal trials should be speedily determined, as reaffirmed in *Parsons v. F.W. Woolworth.*[7] The courts bear collective responsibility for any delay in the fruition of justice. The principle of speedy trials is not confined to criminal proceedings but extends to every species of litigation. The relevant principle of the common law on the subject is embodied in Magna Carta – Justice delayed is justice denied.

1 (1976) 2 All E.R. 865 (H.L.).
2 R.v. Togher, (2001) 3 All E.R. 463 (C.A.).
3 Re A, (2006) 2 All E.R. 1 (C.A.).
4 Osborn v. Parole Board, (2014) 1 All E.R. 369 (S.C.).
5 R. (Ali) v. Director of High Security, (2010) 2 All E.R. 82 (Judge Pelling Q.C.).
6 (1977) 1 All E.R. 620 (C.A.).
7 (1980) 3 All E.R. 456 (D.C.).

 | DOI 10.1163/9789004313736_007

As stated elsewhere, the court has no power at common law to order postponement of publication of judicial proceedings – *Independent Publishing v. A.G.*.[8] This is another affirmation of the principle of open justice. It must, however, be underlined that after the adoption of the European Convention on Human Rights the principles of the common law relevant to open justice have been superseded by its provisions.

In *Kunnath v. The State*[9] the right to an interpreter was likewise acknowledged by the common law, as stated per incuriam.

The right to confront accusers in criminal proceedings is deeply rooted in the common law subject to certain well known exceptions, such as dying declarations in cases of homicide, res gestae and certain statutory exceptions.[10]

A less welcome rule of the common law is the right acknowledged to the court to admit incriminating evidence against the accused by anonymous witnesses.[11]

It is worth noting that in *Re Officer L*[12] the House of Lords reversed a decision of the Court of Appeal to annul the decision of an inquiry in Northern Ireland on the ground that the policemen testified anonymously. The court pointed out that the common law principle to act fairly differs from Article 2 of the Convention on Human Rights. At common law evidence unlawfully obtained was not automatically inadmissible.[13]

Common law recognized the right to be present at a statutory appeal.[14]

What must be clarified is that the development of the common law is possible in relation to procedural law but not so in relation to evidence or substantive law.

The common law acknowledged jurisdiction to postpone passing sentence. Nevertheless, the courts judged that postponing the imposition of sentence is undesirable unless unavoidable. Issue estoppel, despite its significance in civil proceedings, never gained ground in criminal law.

International treaties must be uniformly interpreted: Hence there is no room for the application of the English rules of construction of statutes.[15]

8 (2005) 1 All E.R. 499 (P.C.).
9 (1993) 4 All E.R. 30 (P.C.).
10 R.v. Davis, (2008) 3 All E.R. 46 (H.L.).
11 R.v. Davis (Iain), (2006) 2 Cr.App.R. 444 (32) (C.A.).
12 (2007) 4 All E.R. 965 (H.L.).
13 P.P.S. v. McKee, (2013) 3 All E.R. 365 (S.C.).
14 R. (Gl) v. Secretary of State, (2012) 4 All E.R. 987.
15 Rothmans v. Saudi Arabian Airlines, (1980) 3 All E.R. 359 (C.A.).

At common law murder consisted of the killing of a person motivated by an intention to cause to the victim grievous harm, not to kill as fashioned in due course by statute.[16]

In relation to the crime of conspiracy the following principles were adopted by the House of Lords in *R. v. Cooke*:[17] "If an agreement to commit a crime involves the commission of a statutory offence, then the charge of conspiracy must be founded on the statute. On the other hand, if the agreement to commit a crime does not involve the commission of a statutory offence, then a charge of conspiracy under the common law should be raised. If the conspiracy constituted a statutory as well as a common law offence, it is preferable to base the charge on the statute which prescribes as a rule the sentence that may be imposed, something for which no provision was made at common law".

It must be noted that the courts have no jurisdiction to abolish common law crimes.

In *Davis v. Johnson*[18] the Court of Appeal composed of 5 judges acknowledged power to depart from a previous decision of it if manifestly wrong. The case followed a decision of the House of Lords of 1966 where analogous power was acknowledged to the Judicial Committee of the House. The decision was affirmed by the House of Lords on appeal.[19] The House stressed at the same time that the decision in *Bristol* of 1944 as to stare decisis is still binding on the Court of Appeal. What emerges, to my understanding, is that the Court of Appeal may deviate from a previous decision of it if manifestly wrong.

There is jurisdiction under both common law and equity to order specific performance of a contract provided the claimant is ready to perform his part of the contract.[20]

Foreign law may not be recognized if so inhuman as to defy the hypostasis of law like Nazi legislation depriving Jews of their citizenship and property.[21]

Lastly reference may be made to the assessment of the common law by William Blackstone "the best birthright and noblest inheritance by mankind" (see Hamlyn lecture by Richard O' Sullivan – Inheritance of the Common Law).

From whatever angle one may view the common law and evaluate its diachronic effects the outcome cannot be but positive meeting the needs of

16 Chan Wing-Siu v. R., (1984) 3 All E.R. 877 (P.C).
17 (1986) 2 All E.R. 985 (H.L.).
18 (1978) 1 All E.R. 1132.
19 (1978) 1 All E.R. 1132.
20 Chappell v. The Times Newspapers Ltd., (1975) 2 All E.R. 233 (C.A.).
21 Oppenheimer v. Cattermole, (1975) 1 All E.R. 539 (H.L.).

society by reference to existing knowledge and experience. Its emergence was gradual and its development steady acknowledging in the process human rights and serving the needs of English communities. Worthy of notice on the subject are the observations of F.H. Lawson in his Hamlyn Lecture on the Strength of English Law. "Nevertheless a law should be something of a logical machine and, so long as it avoids over – specialization, it may lay claim to consideration on account of its beauty and elegance". In another passage in the same lecture he says that English unwritten law seems to correspond to Aristotle's conception of natural justice.

CHAPTER 7

Supplementary Reference to Principles of the Common Law

The categories of public interest are not closed.[1]

There is no right to hold property in anticipation of a compensation order. The common law provided no definition of insanity. Insanity embraced acts resulting from malfunction of the brain due to inherent morbid condition of it.[2]

At common law the sheriff was liable for acts of his officers, if they were guilty of insolence or oppressive conduct or goods seized were sold at an undervalue.[3]

In *Blackshaw v. Lord*,[4] it was held that privilege involved (a) legitimate interest of the public to receive information and (b) corresponding duty to make it available.

Breach of the common law right to hold a market is actionable without proof of damage.[5]

The common law rule that a carrier's charge of freight must be paid on delivery without deduction, for any reason, is not confined to carriage of goods by sea but also applies to carriage of goods by road.[6]

The common law recognized the right of the landlord to remove the tenant's fixtures after the end of tenancy – *Mancetter Developments v. Garmonson*.[7]

In *R. v. Sharp*[8] the Court of Appeal identified the sources of common law in the absence of judicial precedent. They are (a) opinion of textbook writers, (b) judicial dicta and reports of Commissions and Legal Committees, (c) analogies with legal systems that share the common law heritage.

Reference must be made to *Associated Japanese Bank v. Credit Du Nord*[9] where it was held in the first place that a mistake must be common to the

1 D. v. N.S.P.C.C., (1977) 1 All E.R. 589 (H.L.).
2 Moore v. Green, (1983) 1 All E.R. 577 (C.A.).
3 Observer Ltd. v. Gordon, (1983) 2 All E.R. 945, (Glidewell J.).
4 (1983) 2 All E.R. 311 (C.A.).
5 Sevenoaks D.C. v. Pattullo & Vinson Ltd., (1984) 1 All E.R. 544 (C.A.).
6 R.H. & D. International v. IAS Air Services, (1984) 2 All E.R. 203, (Neill J.).
7 Mancetter Developments v. Garmanson, (1986) 1 All E.R. 449 (C.A.).
8 (1987) 3 All E.R. 103 (C.A.).
9 (1988) 3 All E.R. 902, (Steyn).

 | DOI 10.1163/9789004313736_008

parties to a contract. Secondly the mistake must render the subject matter of the contract essentially and radically different from that which the parties believed it to be. Lastly a party seeking to rely on mistake must have had reasonable grounds for entertaining belief on which the mistake is founded. Further in *The Great Peace*[10] the court decided that a mistake justified rescission of a contract where the mistake rendered the subject matter of it different from what the parties believed it to be.

The power of a police constable to arrest a person for feared breach of the peace, at common law, can only find justification if the breach of the peace is about to occur or is imminent.[11]

In *Cork v. Rawlins*[12] reference is made to the common law rule exempting from the estate of a bankrupt compensation paid for pain and suffering. The rule had no application in the case of a disabled insured person who received insurance money. Hence the insurance money went to the estate of the disabled person who became bankrupt.

The common law did not recognize a right to a dismissed employee to damages. The right to damages for unfair dismissal is purely statutory subject to its limitations.[13]

In *Delaware Mansions v. Westminster*[14] the House of Lords examined the issue of nuisance arising from the use of land by neighbours. The court stressed that in this field the concern of the common law lies in working out the fair and just content of incidents of a neighbour's duty rather than affixing a label and inferring the extent of the duty from it.

In *Re McKerr*[15] it was acknowledged that the right to life safeguarded by Article 2 of the European Convention on Human Rights had no counterpart at common law.

Oral evidence has always been regarded as the best evidence and should continue to be so regarded. Nonetheless, the common law admitted exceptions to the rule.[16]

The ingredients of the offence of escaping from lawful custody were identified in *R. v. Dhillon*[17] where the court specified the ingredients of the offence of

10 (2002) 4 All E.R. 689 (C.A.).

11 Foulkes v. Chief Constable, (1998) 3 All E.R. 705 (C.A.).

12 (2000) 4 All E.R. 50 (C.A.).

13 Johnson v. Unisys Ltd., (2001) 2 All E.R. 801 (H.L.).

14 (2001) 4 All E.R. 737 (H.L.).

15 (2004) 2 All E.R. 409 (H.L.).

16 Grant v. The State, (2006) C.L.R. 837 Commentary (P.C.).

17 (2006) 1 Cr.App.R. 15.

escaping from custody. They are: (a) Defendant in custody; (b) The custody is lawful; (c) Intentional escape from custody.

In *W.W.F. v. World Wrestling*[18] it was explained that the *Wrothan Park Principle* is a principle of the common law entitling the pursuit of damages without the claimant being able to substantiate financial loss.

The Court in *Halpern v. Halpern (No.2) (Note)*[19] noted that the common law doctrine of duress and the doctrine of equitable estoppel arising from undue influence have much in common. They aim to ensure that justice is done.

The presumption of mens rea in criminal law as an ingredient for the commission of an offence is, as stated in *R. v. M.*,[20] a constitutional principle of great importance. The common law recognized such a presumption. As stated in *Al Rawi v. Security Service*,[21] development of the common law is permissible in relation to procedure not in relation to evidence or substantive law.

The common law recognized a right to recover money paid by mistake – *R. (P.A.G.) v. Secretary of State.*[22]

The common law right to be heard by an administrative authority before taking a decision likely to adversely affect a person can be excluded by reference to legislative provisions authorizing such a course in face of risk to national interest. The right safeguarded by Article 6(1) of the European Convention on Human Rights had a counterpart at common law. The common law recognized that full disclosure of the case of either side to litigation was a common law requirement for a fair trial, applying equally to criminal and civil cases. As noted, only Parliament could sanction otherwise – *Al Rawi v. Security Service.*[23]

The ingredients of the crime of abduction at common law were identified in *R. v. Kayani.*[24] They involve: (a) taking and carrying away A by B; (b) the taking is occasioned by force or fraud; (c) without lawful excuse.

Under the common law the following establishments qualified as charities: (a) Prevention of poverty; (b) advancement of education; (c) advancement of religion; (d) other purposes beneficial to the community – *Independent Schools Council v. Charity Commission.*[25]

---

18 (2008) 1 All E.R. 74 (C.A.).
19 (2007) 3 All E.R. 478 (C.A.).
20 (2010) 4 All E.R. 51 (C.A.).
21 (2010) 4 All E.R. 560 (C.A.).
22 (2011) 1 All E.R. 744 (S.C.).
23 (2012) 1 All E.R. 1 (S.C.).
24 (2012) 2 All E.R. 641.
25 (2012) 1 All E.R. 127 (Upper Tribunal).

In *A. v. British Broadcasting Corporation*[26] it was pointed out that open justice had under the common law and statute its limitations. Therefore, the application of open justice should meet the requirements of the European Convention on Human Rights. On the other hand, in *Kennedy v. Charity Commission*[27] the court recognized that principles of open justice could be developed by the courts as a matter of common law, not dependent on statutory authorization.

The Court of Appeal emphasized in *R. (Mosley) v. Haringcy*[28] that the common law imposes a duty upon a public authority to consult in a broad sense members of the public who will be affected by a decision to be taken. This norm derives from the common law duty to act fairly. This duty would elucidate the manner in which the consultation should be conducted. The requirement of fairness had to be linked to the purposes of consultation.

In *R. v. Chief Magistrate ex p. Choudhury*[29] it was decided that the common law offence of blasphemy was confined at common law to the Christian religion. The right to freedom of religion guaranteed by the European Convention on Human Rights did not impose a duty to criminalize blasphemy respecting any other religion, in this case Islam. At common law a duty of care was owed to a trespasser. This applied also in the case where the trespasser was engaged in a criminal venture. Hence the decision of the trial judge that the defendant who used more violence against the trespasser than was necessary in self-defence was liable to damages. Substantial contributory negligence was ascribed to the plaintiff – *Revill v. Newbery.*[30]

The doctrine of necessity for detention of a person was recognized at common law.

26 (2014) 2 All E.R. 1037 (S.C.).

27 (2014) 2 All E.R. 847.

28 (2015) 1 All E.R. 495 (S.C.).

29 (1991) 1 All E.R. 306 (Q.B.) (Three Judges).

30 (1996) 1 All E.R. 291 (C.A.)

CHAPTER 8

Overview of the Common Law

Customs coincided in the English communities of the Anglo-Saxons, two Teutonic peoples who settled in England in the 5th century CE. The subsequent invasion of the country by the Normans in 1066 and settlement in England left unaffected the development of the common law. The principles of the common law had a twofold purpose – to sustain human rights and ensure orderly life in the communities where they resided. A great step in the process was the identification and written expression of the principles of the common law in judicial decisions.

The courts played a dominant role in the identification of the principles and rules of the common law and its development to meet new needs emerging from the evolution of society and advances in the field of technology. In so doing the courts endeavoured to gear the process by reference to the fundamental norms of the common law. In due course societies became more complex, a fact that led to the expansion of the common law to meet new needs of society. Sequentially the common law found expression in judicial decisions thereafter often referred to as judge made law.

The course of expansion of the common law was gradual, never assuming revolutionary characteristics. English judges never assumed the role of law makers. They confined themselves to the development of the common law never wearing the mantle of law makers. As legislation increased in the process of time becoming the principal instrument of addressing the needs of society, questions arose respecting the co-existence of legislation and the common law. The legislature never abrogated or sought to abolish or play down the existence of the common law, recognizing that it reflects the inborn notions of the people about justice and the law. Hence, as repeatedly decided, legislation does not abolish or override principles and rules of the common law unless this is specifically stated in the law or derives by inescapable implication. This was stressed in very clear terms by the Judicial Committee of the House of Lords – *R. (Rottman) v. Commissioner of Police.*[1]

Judges kept a proper balance between legislative provisions and common law principles originally deriving, as already noted, from the common will of the people of England, subsequently supplemented by the courts to address

1 (2002) 2 All E.R. 865 (H.L.).

 | DOI 10.1163/9789004313736_009

new needs of the people. Law was identified as the supreme authority. In ancient Greece law was known as "despot law".

Legislation, common law and sequentially equity can be identified as providing the constitutional framework of English law. England never had a written constitution except periodic declarations about fundamental rights, such as the Magna Carta of 1215 and the Bills of Rights of 1629 and 1689.

Following the tragic events of the 2nd World War offending humanity to the core, the Universal Declaration of Human Rights of 1948 was a monumental event in the history of humanity. It was followed by regional conventions adopting many of its principles, such as the European Convention on Human Rights and conventions to the same effect in America and Africa. Fundamental human rights were embodied into the constitutions of many states. The Constitution of Cyprus adopts human rights in a very comprehensive way, following in many respects the European Convention on Human Rights albeit in a stricter form. The European Convention on Human Rights was adopted as part of the domestic law of England in 1998 and put into force in the year 2000.

The adoption of a Code of human rights by European countries and other parts of the world has enriched the law in major respects, one being that human rights are given universal dimensions. Human rights are identified with human nature independently of ethnic, religious, colour, sexual origin or physique.

As earlier indicated, the common law recognized a number of human rights, referred to in some judicial decisions as constitutional rights, meaning inalienable. In my view respect of humanity by the common law was one of the principal reasons for the adoption of English law in former British colonies after independence and this, despite the ill and in certain respects catastrophic effects of English rule in the colonies.

Justice and fairness as well as pressing social needs were the guide to the extension of the common law but there were limits to it. Its extension in new areas was not permissible when a subject was covered comprehensively by a statute. If so, recourse either to the common law or equity on the ground that it would produce a fairer result was not permissible.

On the other hand, as repeatedly decided by the courts, the common law is not abrogated by statute unless the subject matter of the rule is the subject of a specific legislative provision. As a matter of course the courts should not extend fundamental principles in areas where Parliament had made recent and detailed intervention. The common law has recognized or acknowledged fundamental human rights regarded as identical to constitutional rights, such as freedom of expression and freedom of the press.

The expansion of the common law to meet changing circumstances and current reality was repeatedly proclaimed as part of the constitutional role of the courts in addition to interpreting the law.

The common law evolved, as correctly indicated by Lord Roger, by making pragmatic and incremental development of the law, provided always that changes were consistent with the basic principles of the common law. Logic was to a great extent a guide in the development of the common law. The common law developed by the formulation of general principles, not by identification of specific rules to resolve a specific matter at issue.

CHAPTER 9

Origin and Principles of Equity

Historically equity emanated from the Crown assuming powers to remedy injustice. In due course the grant of equitable relief was assigned to the Lord Chancellor who in turn set up courts endowed with jurisdiction to administer equity.

By the Judicature Acts of 1873 and 1876 courts of equity became part of the structure of ordinary courts enhancing the role of equity in the administration of justice. In fact one of the divisions of the High Court – the Chancery Division – primarily deals with cases referable to the principles of equity.

As earlier indicated, equity incorporates pananthropic law. Secular law addresses as a rule societal order conferring rights and imposing duties on members of society, a process that led to the formation and sequential application of the common law. With the development of the democratic system of government and allocation of legislative powers to representatives of the people the common and statute law established a comprehensive code of rights, duties and governmental powers. Yet it is difficult, if not impossible, to address apriori all the needs of justice, many of which emerge in unforeseeable circumstances. Equity is meant to fill the gaps enabling the court to do justice whenever existing rules make no provision for remedying what is perceived as unjust. In other words, equity is akin to natural law, that is to say, the law that befits justice. Hence acts contrary to justice are likely to be declared void but until so declared, the decision is heeded by law – *Calvin v. Carr.*[1]

Equitable rights and defences operate on the conscience of the plaintiff – *James Graham & Co. v. Southgate Sands.*[2] Equity, as judicially declared, is not a computer. It operates, as indicated, on the conscience of a person but is not influenced by sentimentality.[3] Equity treats as done that which ought to have been done.[4] In *Simaan Co. v. Pilkington Glass (No. 2)*[5] it was pronounced: "Just as equity remedied the inadequacies of the common law, so has the law of torts filled gaps left by other causes of action where the interests of justice so required".

---

1 (1979) 2 All E.R. 440 (P.C.).

2 (1985) 2 All E.R. 344 (C.A.).

3 Winkworth Edward v. Baron Development Co., (1987) 2 All E.R. 114 (H.L.).

4 Harfela v. Royal Trust Co. of Canada, (1985) 2 All E.R. 966 (H.L.).

5 (1988) 1 All E.R. 791 (C.A.).

 | DOI 10.1163/9789004313736_010

If there are two creditors and they have (a) a common property for security and (b) one of them had a second property as security, the principle of *Marshalling* that the creditor who had two properties as security should realize the security over which the second creditor had no claim[6] finds application.

As stressed in *M.C.C. Proceeds v. Lehman Bros.*,[7] neither the Judicature Acts nor procedural changes transform equitable interests into legal rights. One can say that equity is the guardian of conscientious conduct.

In *Banner Homes v. Luff Developments Ltd.*[8] reference is made to Australian commentators who said: "Equity must retain its inherent flexibility and capacity to adjust to new situations by reference to the mainsprings of equitable jurisdiction". Furthermore it was said that "equity must never be deferred by the absence of precise analogy, provided the principle invoked is sound". It must be clarified that it is no business of equity to afford relief from a bad bargain. As stated, only in exceptional circumstances could equity relieve a party from an unconscionable bargain. In *Marcic v. Thames Water*[9] after reference to *Lopez Ostra v. Spain*[10] the Court decided that equitable damages is the means to compensate a person for non pecuniary damages. Moreover in *Douglas v Hello! Ltd.*[11] it was clarified that the right to privacy is established by the European Convention on Human Rights and not as an aspect of equitable confidence.

Although equity will not help a volunteer, it will not strive officially to defeat a gift. In the same case it was decided that it was immaterial that assets were held by only one of the trustees. He was bound in conscience to hold them for all of them.[12]

The decision in *Twinsectra v. Vardley*[13] dealt with what amounts to dishonesty in equity. Proof of dishonesty required two things: (a) Dishonest conduct by the standards of reasonable and honest people and (b) awareness that by these standards the conduct of a person was dishonest.

Although equity will not assist a volunteer, it applies a benevolent construction towards a gift – *Pennington v. Wane.*[14]

6 Highbury Pension Fund v. Zirfin Investments, (2014) 1 All E.R. 674 (C.A.).

7 (1998) 4 All E.R. 675 (C.A.).

8 (2000) 2 All E.R. 117 (C.A.).

9 (2001) 3 All E.R. 698 (Richard Harery J.).

10 (1995) 20 E.H.R.R. 277.

11 (2001) 2 All E.R. 289 (C.A.).

12 Choithram v. Pagarani, (2001) 2 All E.R. 482 (P.C.).

13 (2002) 2 All E.R. 377 (H.L.).

14 Pennington v. Waine, (2002) 4 All E.R. 215 (C.A.).

Just and equitable included whatever justice and equity included – *Dunnachie v. Kingston – upon – Hull.*[15]

Equity rendered a voluntary disposition made by the disposer under a mistake of an existing or preexisting fact voidable; unlike common law a mistake in equity made the transaction voidable, not void.[16] The equitable jurisdiction to set aside a disposition for mistake cannot be invoked where the transaction gave rise to unforeseen consequences, not an effect of the mistake – *(Pitt) v. Holt.*[17]

For the defendant to invoke laches as a defence there must be some detrimental effect to his rights that on a balance of justice warranted refusal of relief. The court also pointed out that the defence of laches must substantially be founded on equitable principles – *Fisher v. Brooker.*[18]

Equity acknowledges that mistake like fraud gives rise to an extended limitation period.[19] Tracing in equity depended not on the actual imposition of an equitable charge but on equity's capacity to impose such a charge – *El Ajou v. Dollar Land Holdings (No.2).*[20]

Under Section 37(1) of the Supreme Court Act of 1981 power was bestowed upon the court to order equitable execution to receive debts of a judgment creditor provided the court was satisfied that the third party debtor could be adequately protected against double jeopardy.[21]

The maxims of equity reflect in a wide sense the objects and purposes of equity. They are cited below:-

1. Equity will not suffer a wrong to be without a remedy;
2. Equity follows the law;
3. Where there is equal equity, the law shall prevail;
4. Where the equities are equal, the first in time shall prevail;
5. He who seeks equity must do equity;
6. He who comes into equity must come with clean hands;
7. Delay defeats equities, or, equity aids the vigilant and not the indolent;
8. Equality is equity;
9. Equity looks to the intent rather than to the form;

15 (2004) 2 All E.R. 501 (C.A.).

16 Re Griffiths (decd), (2008) 2 All E.R. 654 (Lewison J.).

17 (P.H.) v. Holt, (2011) 2 All E.R. 450 (C.A.).

18 (2009) 4 All E.R. 789 (H.L.).

19 F.I.I. Claimants v. R.C.C.(2012) 3 All E.R. 909 (S.C.).

20 El Ajou v. Dollar Land Holdings (No. 2), (1995) 2 All E.R. 213 (Robert Walker J.).

21 Lonrho plc. v. Fayed (No. 2), (1991) 4 All E.R. 961 (Millett J.).

10. Equity looks on that as done which ought to be done;
11. Equity imputes an intention to fulfill an obligation;
12. Equity acts in personam.

Equity does not interfere to grant relief in commercial agreements – *Mardorf Peach v. Attica Sea Carriers Corporation.*[22]

In *Patel v. Ali*[23] the court held that where a party acted extortionately, oppressively or coercively towards the other party to the contract, the court in fairness will set aside the transaction.

It is worth citing the following passage from the judgment of Browne – Wilkinson, L.J., in *James Graham & Co. v. Southgate Sands*:[24] "Equitable rights and defences operate and operate only on the conscience of the plaintiff". In *Dunnachi v. Kingston – upon – Hull*[25] the court observed that the concept of just and equitable included whatever justice and equity encompassed.

22 (1976) 2 All E.R. 249 (C.A.).
23 (1984) 1 All E.R. 978 (Goulding J.).
24 (1985) 2 All E.R. 344 (C.A.).
25 (2004) 2 All E.R. 501 (C.A.).

CHAPTER 10

Instantiation of the Application of the Principles of Equity

By its nature the application of equity cannot be confined to any specific field or fields. What the case law brings to the fore are areas where the principles of equity found application instantiating the relief afforded. Naturally the Judiciary is responsible for the identification of the principles of equity and their application in the various domains of human conflict. If anything can be discerned from the approach of the courts to the invocation and application of equity is that it is expansive, treating equity as the embodiment of universal rules of justice, synonymous with fairness, as the guide to the resolution of disputes between human beings, including corporate organizations.

Legal precedent is certainly important but does not curtail the stream of equity having at its core conscience, barring unconscionable conduct in the transaction of the affairs of humanity. The elements of conscientious behaviour and expectation of analogous behavior from fellow human beings and legal bodies, organizations or institutions are nowadays incorporated in a general form in fundamental codes and constitutions.

Below we shall refer to cases where judicial decisions on principles of equity found application. We may begin with breach of confidence.

Human passions often arising from material interest are generally what divorces man from reason that should be the only guide in every sphere of life. Human weaknesses, including disobedience of ethical rules, are often what lead human beings astray.

 | DOI 10.1163/9789004313736_011

CHAPTER 11

Breach of Confidence

Confidence is a very delicate aspect of human relations. Breach of it justifies equitable protection and relief. An injunction is the appropriate relief for breach of confidence prohibiting the passing off or use of confidential information.

An agreement between parties in a confidential relationship, including the relationship between solicitor and client, cannot be upheld unless the person claiming to enforce the contract can prove affirmatively that the person standing in such a confidential position has disclosed, without reservation all the information in his possession and can further show that the transaction involving confidentiality was a fair one, with regard to all circumstances – B.C.C. I. *v. Aboody*.[1]

A solicitor stands in a confidential relationship to a person to whom he renders legal advice, as decided in *Halifax Mortgage Societies v. Stepsky*.[2] If a question of disclosure of confidential information received from "A" by "B" in the absence of express consent from "A" to disclose it, the solicitor must disengage from representation of a party.

A solicitor appointed by a bank to explain to a wife what standing as surety to her husband entails, must explain to her that her decision must be voluntary, free of any pressure or misrepresentation from her husband. *In Royal Bank of Scotland v. Etridge*[3] a solicitor thus appointed failed to carry out his duty. Sequentially notice of presumed undue influence exerted by the husband on the wife was attributed to the Bank.

In *Murray v. Yorkshire Fund Managers*[4] the court resolved that in order to succeed in an action for breach of confidence it had to be shown that (a) apart from contract, (b) the information had the necessary quality of confidence about it, (c) it had been imparted in circumstances importing an obligation of confidence, (d) there was an unauthorized use of it to the detriment of the party communicating it.

A person who establishes that an agreement should be set aside on account of breach of confidence is entitled in equity to damages for a sum equal to the

1 (1992) 4 All E.R. 955 (C.A.).

2 (1995) 4 All E.R. 656 (Edward Nugee sitting as Deputy Chancery Judge).

3 (1997) 3 all E.R. 629 (C.A.).

4 (1998) 2 All E.R. 1015 (C.A.).

 | DOI 10.1163/9789004313736_012

value of the interest of the plaintiff in the property before the transaction was set aside.[5]

In *Barclays Bank Plc v. O'Brien & Another*[6] the court examined the circumstances under which a surety for a debt of her husband procured by pressure, undue influence or misrepresentation would be held unenforceable. If the relation between debtor and surety is known by the creditor, the wife will be relieved of her contractual obligation. It was stressed that the creditor must ensure that the wife had a proper understanding of the transaction. A creditor who obtains security from the debtor's wife ought to take reasonable steps, such as advising her to take independent advice, or if she declines to do so, offering a fair explanation of the obligations that the wife is undertaking before she signed as surety. Under the ordinary principles of equity a wife who has been induced by her husband by undue influence or misrepresentation to stand as surety for his debt has an equitable right to relinquish any liability vis-à-vis third parties if either the husband was acting as the third party's agent or the third party had actual or constructive notice of the facts leading to the wife becoming surety of a debt of her husband. On the other hand, the equitable right of a wife to avoid obligations as surety of her husband, induced by his influence, is not applicable respecting a third party who had no actual or constructive knowledge of the influence exerted upon the surety by her husband.

5 Mahoney v. Purnell, (1996) 3 All E.R. 61 (May J.).

6 (1992) 4 All E.R. 983 (C.A.).

CHAPTER 12

Undue Influence

The exercise of undue influence has as a background the dependence of "A" on "B" and sequentially the amenity of "B" to draw "A" into disadvantageous agreements. Such influence, as the case law suggests, is likely to be exerted by a husband over his wife. As women gain progressively higher social and marital status, a reflection of the equality of human beings, independently of sex, the scope for the exercise of undue influence by husband over his wife is, I dare say, lessened.

Where a person seeks to set aside a transaction for presumed undue influence (a) he/she has to show that the transaction was manifestly disadvantageous to him/her and (b) make restitution in respect of all that the person had obtained from the transaction.

The principles governing the undertaking by a wife of obligations to a bank for her husband's debts and their applicability were itemized in *Royal Bank* (*supra*) as follows: (1) When the wife acts through a solicitor, the bank is not ordinarily put on enquiry and is not required to take any steps to determine her voluntariness in undertaking the obligations to the bank; (2) When the wife does not act through a solicitor, it is normally sufficient if the bank urges her to obtain independent legal advice; (3) When a solicitor gives advice to a wife, she is presumed to act independently of her husband or anybody else; (4) If the bank nominates a solicitor to advise a wife, he is regarded as acting as her solicitor; (5) The bank is not fixed with imputed knowledge of what the solicitor knows; (6) The bank is under no obligation to question the sufficiency of the solicitor's advice.

 | DOI 10.1163/9789004313736_013

CHAPTER 13

Cause of Action and Issue Estoppel

Finality in the resolution of disputes and the litigation associated therewith is vital as to the definition of one's rights and obligations knowledge of which is essential for planning one's life.

Cause of action and issue estoppel ruling out relitigation of decided issues and causes is an equitable principle of long standing. The subject is debated at length by the House of Lords in *Johnson v. Gore Wood & Co.*[1]

Issue and cause of action estoppel arise from the final resolution of a judicial cause before the court, as underlined in *Buehler v. Chronos Richardson.*[2] Finality of litigation underlines these principles of equity. Cause of action estoppel arises only if the cause of action in earlier proceedings is identical with the cause of action in subsequent proceedings. The two causes must be identical. Estoppel arises also in relation to issues upon which the cause of action is founded.

In *Virgin Atlantif v. Zodiac*[3] it was stressed that except in rare cases when this could lead to injustice, action estoppel arises also in respect of all matters that could be legitimately raised in the action. As clarified in *R (Beresford) v. Sanderland Council*,[4] issue estoppel arises whenever an issue is a relevant part of a litigated cause of action and the same issue arises for consideration in subsequent proceedings concerned with another cause of action to which the issue is relevant.

It must be noted that equity recognized jurisdiction to make an order of disclosure by a non-party in a case involving wrongful conduct affecting a claimant's right.[5] It must be clarified that damages awarded in judicial proceedings merge with the cause of action.[6] Moreover cause of action estoppel is applicable to ordinary judicial proceedings. It has no application in proceedings before employment tribunals – *Ako v. Rothschild Assell Management.*[7]

1 (2001) 1 All E.R. 481, 494.
2 (1998) 2 All E.R. 960 (C.A.).
3 (2012) 4 All E.R. 715 (S.C.).
4 (2001) 4 All E.R. 565 (C.A.).
5 Ashworth v. M.G.N., (2001) 1 All E.R. 991 (C.A.).
6 Fraser v. H.L.M.A.D., (2007) 1 All E.R. 383 (C.A.).
7 Ako v. Rothschild Assell Management, (2002) 2 All E.R. 693 (C.A.).

 DOI 10.1163/9789004313736_014

It must be clarified that cause of action and issue estoppel as distinct from res judicata has no application in criminal law [*D.P.P. Hamphys* (1977) A.C. 1(H.L.)]. Res judicata lays down that no one should be put in jeopardy twice of being convicted and punished for the same offence twice. (Autrefois acquit – autrefois convict)

CHAPTER 14

Trusts

The word "trust" has a multitude of meanings. Having faith and confidence in statements and contracts with a fellow human being is a classical example. As a noun it has the meaning of an establishment designed to leave property to others entrusting its administration to trustees, the confidants who undertake a duty to administer the property in good faith bearing in mind the principles governing their assignment. In *Sieff v. Fox*[1] the court decided that it is a rule of equity that the trustee has, in the exercise of his duty, a responsibility to take into account relevant considerations in the exercise of his powers to the exclusion of irrelevant considerations and matters.

A liquidator stands in essence in the position of a trustee. In *Re Exchange Securities and Commodities Ltd.*[2] it was underlined that a liquidator stands essentially in the position of a trustee, explaining that he is not bound by any estoppel between creditor and company.

In human exchanges a trust may arise in circumstances warranting the interposition of equity. The case of *Eves v. Eves*[3] provides an example. The husband told his wife, aged 19, that when she became 21 years old, the house registered in his name would be registered in the name of both of them. Meantime his wife did a lot to improve the house. The husband went back on his word. The court held that a constructive trust was created binding the husband to register half of the house in the name of his wife.

In *Re Cleaver (deceased)*[4] it was held that if two persons make wills upon a previous understanding as to benefits that will be granted, equity will impose a constructive trust, charging the legal owner to distribute the property upon what had been agreed. The principles of equitable compensation do not vary according on the nature of the trust but the scope of the trust could have a bearing on the appropriate relief in the event of breach.

There is a variety of trusts defined by reference to their origin. Notably statutory trusts created by virtue of statutory authority, express trusts set up by individuals and further resulting trusts imposed by law. Vesting land gradually

1 (2005) 3 All E.R. 693 (Lloyd, L.J.).

2 (1987) 2 All E.R. 272 (Harman).

3 (1975) 3 All E.R. 768 (C.A.).

4 (1981) 2 All E.R. 1018 (Nourse, J.).

 | DOI 10.1163/9789004313736_015

conferred to the transferee back to the transferor where the transferee curries out the obligations undertaken. Constructive trusts where the Court in the interests of justice regards it unconscionable for the owner to keep the whole property to the exclusion of the claimant (see *Law of Trusts and Trustees, by Underhill and Hayton, 17th edition p. 71*).

CHAPTER 15

Duress

Duress and related issues in equity are equated with fraud or undue influence. A person subjected to duress (re contract) is entitled to relief despite the fact that he might have signed the agreement in the absence of compulsion.[1]

In *Halpen v. Halpen* (*No.2* (*Note*))[2] the court propounded the view that the common law doctrine of duress and the doctrine of equitable estoppel arising from undue influence have much in common. Both aim to ensure that justice is done.

Release from obligations (undertaken) to "B" will in equity be ineffective if the facts bearing on the release are dishonestly withheld.[3] There must be a causal link between the receipt of money and the change of position such that it would make it inequitable to return the money to the owner.[4]

A defrauded plaintiff has in equity a right to trace property and the courts will aid him in the pursuit.[5]

1 Barton v. Armstrong, (1975) 2 All E.R. 465 (P.C.).
2 (2007) 3 All E.R. 478 (C.A.).
3 B.B.C.I. v. Ali, (2000) 2 All E.R. 51 (C.A.).
4 Scottish Equitable v. Derby, (2000) 3 All E.R. 793, (Harrison, J.).
5 Bankers Trust Co. v. Shapira, (1980) 3 All E.R. 353 (C.A.).

 | DOI 10.1163/9789004313736_016

CHAPTER 16

Specific Performance

Specific performance is an equitable remedy available to the court empowering it to order the execution of a contract where its subject matter is identifiable as in the case of the sale of immovable property. Equity bars specific performance not only when there was an active failure to disclose but also when the vendor made an innocent representation when true facts were within his knowledge – *Walker v. Boyle.*[1] Equity acknowledges partial performance as a legitimate remedy. Thus where "A" represents to "B" that he is the owner of property and agrees to give first mortgage, the court may order partial performance after balancing the interests of third parties respecting ownership.

Specific performance emerged as an equitable remedy where the remedy of damages at common law could not do justice to the claimant. Specific performance relates to the object of an agreement which must be in existence at the time when a civil action is raised, land as a rule but not exclusively. The object may be a chattel or chattels.

1 (1982) 1 All E.R. 634 (Dillon, L.J.).

 | DOI 10.1163/9789004313736_017

CHAPTER 17

Set Off

In judicial proceedings where a cross claim is directly connected with the subject matter of the claim, it would be manifestly unjust to allow the claimant to recover without taking into account the cross claim.[1]

There is, as it emerges, a right of set off in equity of an unliquidated claim for damages. A claim by a shipowner for freight or his assignees, can be set off by a charterer's claim arising from subsequent repudiation.[2]

Generally a demand for unliquidated damages could give rise to an equitable set off, as acknowledged in *British Anzani v. International Marine*.[3] It must be clarified that for equitable set off to apply the claim of the defendant must be directly connected with the plaintiff's claim.

In *Geldof Metal Constructive N.V. v. Simon Carves Ltd.*[4] the court cited with approval the definition of Lord Denning of the equitable principle of set off: "Cross claims.... so closely connected with plaintiff's demands for damages that it would be manifestly unjust to allow him to enforce payment without taking into account the cross claim".

It emerges that equity acknowledges partial performance as a legitimate remedy.

1 Sim v. Rotherham Metropolitan B.C., (1986) 3 All E.R. 387 (Scott, J.).

2 Colonial Bank v. European Grain Ltd., (1988) 3 All E.R. 233 (C.A.).

3 (1979) 2 All E.R. 1063 (Forbes, J.).

4 (2010) 4 All E.R. 847 (C.A.).

 | DOI 10.1163/9789004313736_018

CHAPTER 18

Equitable Assignment

Equitable assignment has consequences in law. Thus in *Swiss Bank Corporation v. Lloyds Bank*[1] the court held that a contract, for valuable consideration, to keep a fund available for the repayment of a loan creates an interest over the land by way of equitable assignment if the contract is one for which equity would decree specific performance.

In *Three Rivers D.C. v. Bank of England*[2] it was decided that in an agreement to assign a legal chose, the assignee became in equity the owner and controller of the legal chose and was entitled to sue for the recovery of the chose although as a matter of practice he is required by the court to join the assignor as plaintiff or, if he refuses to consent, to join him as a defendant.

In *Weddell v. S. A. Pearce & Major*[3] it was declared that an equitable assignee may sue in his name but cannot recover damages or seek a perpetual injunction without joining the assignor as a party to the suit.

1 (1979) 2 All E.R. 853 (Browne – Wilkinson, L.J.).

2 (1995) 4 All E.R. 312 (C.A.).

3 (1987) 3 All E.R. 624 (Scott, J.).

 | DOI 10.1163/9789004313736_019

CHAPTER 19

Laches

Delay which is sufficient to prevent a party from obtaining an equitable remedy is called or termed Laches (see *Partridge V Patridge* (*1894*) *1 Ch. 351, 359–360*).

Laches can only bar equitable relief, not a statutory right. For a defendant to invoke laches, there must have been a detrimental event to his rights which "in a balance of justice" justifies refusal of relief. The defence of laches must substantially be founded on equitable principles – *Fisher v. Brooker.*[1] For the equitable principle of laches to be established the alleged prejudice must be founded on loss, not as a theoretical possibility but as a real event. Speculations and assumptions are not enough. The doctrine of laches is applied by reference to the particular circumstances of a case, including (a) the period of delay and the extent to which defendant's position has been prejudiced by the delay and (b) the extent to which the prejudice was caused by actions of the plaintiff. What must be clarified is that equity does not interfere to grant relief in commercial agreements.

Equitable damages, as previously noticed, is the means to compensate non pecuniary damages.

---

1 (2009) 4 All E.R. 789 (H.L.).

 | DOI 10.1163/9789004313736_020

CHAPTER 20

Subrogation

In *Orakpo v. Mansion Investments Ltd.*[1] the court clarified that subrogation does not rest on contract but is a principle of equity to avoid injustice.

In the case of *Hobbs v. Marlowe*[2] the court dealt with the claim of one insurance company to be reimbursed by another. It was decided that no subrogation could arise. There was, as stated, no extension of subrogation regarding one insurance company and another. There is, the court observed, a difference between the assignment of rights of action and the fruits of an action.

A decision where equitable principles did not get the upper hand is *Blathwayt v. Lord Cawley*.[3] A testator provided in his will that a beneficiary thereunder would forfeit his right if he became a Roman Catholic. He did become a Roman Catholic but claimed his right under the will of the testator. The court decided that although courts must move with contemporary concepts of non discrimination, this must be balanced with deeply rooted principles of testamentary disposition. Hence the claim of the Roman Catholic was dismissed.

In *Barclays Bank v. Boutter*[4] it was decided that where a party alleged that an agreement was signed by misrepresentation, it was for the claimant to prove that he did not have notice of misrepresentation. Similar principles were adopted in *Dunbar Bank v. Nadeem*.[5]

1 (1977) 1 All E.R. 666 (C.A.).
2 (1977) 2 All E.R. 241 (H.L.).
3 (1975) 3 All E.R. 625 (H.L.).
4 (1997) 2 All E.R. 1002 (C.A.).
5 (1997) 2 All E.R. 253 (Robert Englehart, Q.C.).

 | DOI 10.1163/9789004313736_021

CHAPTER 21

Estoppel

The Concise Oxford Dictionary (1990's Ed.) defines the verb "estop" as follows: "Law bar or preclude, esp. by estoppel". The noun "estoppel" is thus defined in the same dictionary: "Law – the principle which precludes a person from asserting something contrary to what is implied by a previous action or statement of that person or by a previous pertinent judicial determination". Estoppel is a principle of justice of equity, as affirmed in *Moorgate Mercantile v. Twitchings*[1]; *Natwest v. Somer International.*[2] In every respect the term "equity" is synonymous with justice. As a rule estoppel arises whenever a representee has relied on a representation, thereby altering his position, by going ahead with a transaction – *Brikom Investments Ltd. v. Carr.*[3] It must be underlined that estoppel as a remedy originated at common law. Equity adopted it and greatly enriched the doctrine extending it to meet the needs of justice (see Snell's Equity, 30th edition p. 649 et seq.).

In *Greasley v. Cooke*[4] it was decided that there is a presumption that a representee acted on a promise made. It must be stressed that for a representation to give rise to estoppel it must be unequivocal.[5]

The sufferance of detriment by the representee although a corollary in most cases of a misrepresentation is not an invariable prerequisite for founding equitable estoppel. In the same case it was decided that buyers are not estopped from rejecting goods a short time after their receipt. This is not inequitable.

Two prerequisites must be satisfied to found an equitable estoppel: (a) clear representation that the representor will not insist on the enforcement of strict legal rights and (b) in the circumstances it would be inequitable not to allow the representee who has been so influenced by the representation as to warrant the intervention of equity.

In *Avon C.C. v. Howlett*[6] it was held that estoppel by representation being a rule of evidence operated in appropriate circumstances so as to prevent the representor from averring facts contrary to his representation. In the same

1 (1975) 3 All E.R. 314 (C.A.).
2 (2002) 1 All E.R. 198 (C.A.).
3 (1979) 2 All E.R. 753 (C.A.).
4 (1980) 3 All E.R. 710 (C.A.).
5 See also China-Pacific S.A. v. Food Corporation of India, (1980).3 All E.R. 556 (C.A.).
6 (1983) 1 All E.R. 1073 (C.A.).

 | DOI 10.1163/9789004313736_022

case it was held that a person paying money by mistake is not stopped from claiming it. On the other hand, in *Langdale v. Darly*[7] a defendant was estopped from withdrawing a statement that there was no impropriety on the part of the plaintiff because that would cause detriment to the plaintiff and delay in the proceedings.

Promises may emerge from word or conduct. Unfairness may result from the use of the rules of a company in a manner that equity regards as unfair – *Re a Company*.[8]

Representations as to an existing state of affairs bars the representor from escaping from them – *Ismail v. Polish Ocean Lines.*[9] Estoppel is a private law concept. Consequently it was decided that it is unhelpful to introduce private law concepts into planning law.

There has been considerable expansion of the application of estoppel in recent years, as pointed out in *Habib Bank Ltd. v. Habib Bank A.G. Zurich.*[10] An instance of this tendency is the affirmation of a tenancy by estoppel. Another noticeable example is the expansion of the application of estoppel to companies, as indicated in *Amalgamated Investment v. Texas Commerce.*[11]

In *Janred Properties Ltd. v. ENIT*[12] it was affirmed that a contract void because of failure to adhere to the necessary formalities, soon remedied, bound the parties, estopping the defendant from denying the agreement. On the other hand, it is no business of equity to afford a party relief from a bad bargain. Only in exceptional circumstances would equity relieve a party from an unconscionable agreement – *Charion Ltd. v. National Provident Institution.*[13]

Lastly estoppel may arise in relation to a document entitled a "deed" even if some of the statutory formalities are not complied with, as were not complied with in the particular case respecting attestation of signatures – *Re Al Fawwaz.*[14]

Summing up, in relation to the hypostasis and role of estoppel one can venture the view that it is playing a dominant part in mitigating the rigours of strict application of the law where so to do postulating rules of equity as superior law, is an expression of pananthropic justice. The decision in *Calvin v. Carr*[15] depicts the essence of equity. It was held that decisions contrary to natural justice are void but, until so declared, they are heeded by the law.

7 (1982) 2 All E.R. 129 (H.L.).
8 (1999) 2 All E.R. 961 (H.L.).
9 (1976) 1 All E.R. 902 (C.A.).
10 (1981) 2 All E.R. 650 (C.A.).
11 (1981) 3 All E.R. 577 (C.A.).
12 (1989) 2 All E.R. 444 (C.A.).
13 (2000) 2 All E.R. 265 – (Romer, J.).
14 (2101) 3 All E.R. 149 (C.A.).
15 (1979) 2 All E.R. 540.

CHAPTER 22

Promissory Estoppel

Promissory estoppel renders a promisor bound by his promise notwithstanding the absence of legal obligation.

In *Evenden v. Guildford City Football Club*[1] the court held that a promise by a football club to a footballer that his employment would be continuous was found to be binding notwithstanding the absence of a contract. As Lord Denning giving the judgment of the court pointed out the representation was intended to be binding and intended to be acted upon. Also in *Argy Trading v. Lapid Developments*[2] it was decided that the representation must be intended to affect the legal relations of the parties.

The decision of the Privy Council in *Maharaj v. Chand*[3] is significant for two reasons. It supports (a) that the interest acquired by a promissory estoppel is personal and (b) the doctrine of promissory estoppel is now firmly established although its frontiers are still worked out. The promise, it must be stressed, must be express by word or conduct. It must be intended to affect the legal relations of the parties (contractual or otherwise) and sequentially the representee alters his positions to his detriment (see Tool Metal Manufacturing Co Ltd v Tungsten Electric Co Ltd 1955 1WLR) 761, 764. see also Snell's Equity, 30th edition 2000, page 634, para 39-08 until 39-10.

1 (1975) 3 All E.R. 269 (C.A.).

2 (1977) 3 All E.R. 785 (Croom-Johnson, L.J.).

3 (1986) 3 All E.R. 107 (P.C.).

 | DOI 10.1163/9789004313736_023

CHAPTER 23

Proprietary Estoppel

Promissory estoppel aims to stop the promisor from escaping from his promise. Proprietary estoppel aims to confer rights to property arising from promise. In *Crabb v. Arun D.C.*[1] Lord Denning pronounced that the basis of proprietary as well as promissory estoppel is the interposition of equity. One may say that in both cases estoppel has the same purpose, notably to hold a person bound by his representation, including representations regarding the conferment of property.

In *Taylor Fashions v. Liverpool Victoria Trustees Co.*[2] the prerequisites for substantiating proprietary estoppel were itemised: (a) there must be acquiescence or encouragement, (b) proprietary estoppel is not dependent on awareness by the parties of their rights and consequential readiness by the representor to compromise them. The same principles are adopted in *Amalgamated Investment v. Texas Commerce.*[3] In the latter case it was indicated that a gratuitous promise may result in estoppel if it would otherwise be unconscionable by the promisor not to fulfill his promise.

In *Western Fish Products v. Penwith D.C.*[4] the history of proprietary estoppel is reviewed. It is stressed that the application of proprietary estoppel is limited to proprietary rights in land. Estoppel, it was said, cannot be raised to prevent the exercise of a statutory discretion or to prevent or excuse the performance of a statutory duty.

In *Re Basham (decd)*[5] the Judge held that proprietary estoppel arises whenever "A" acted to his detriment to the knowledge and encouragement of "B" that "A" has or will be given a right. If the right relates to the future, it constitutes a species of constructive trust.

The principles governing proprietary estoppel are discussed at length by Carnwath J. in *Gillett v. Holt.*[6] To begin with, the Judge stresses that proprietary estoppel is an acknowledged principle of the law of equity. Thereafter he examined the principles relevant to its emergence: (1) to found proprietary

1 (1975) 3 All E.R. 865 (C.A.).
2 (1981) 1 All E.R. 897, (Oliver, J.).
3 (1981) 1 All E.R. 923 (Robert Goff).
4 (1981) 2 All E.R. 204 (C.A.).
5 (1987) 1 All E.R. 405 (Edward Nagee, Q.C., sitting as a Deputy Judge of H.C.)
6 (1998) 3 All E.R. 917.

 DOI 10.1163/9789004313736_024

estoppel a binding contract is not necessary; (2) the overriding principle is that a party must be held to his representations if it would be unconscionable to do otherwise. Furthermore it must be established that the representee acted to his detriment owing to reliance on the representation to the knowledge of the maker of the representation; (3) the representation must take the form of an irrevocable promise.

A case illuminating the context of proprietary estoppel is *Thorner v. Major*.[7] For a proprietary estoppel to be created it was enough that the meaning conveyed by the promisor had been understood by the addressee as intended to be seriously taken, i.e. as an assurance that it could be seriously taken. If the promisee acted upon the given promise to his detriment, the requisites of proprietary estoppel are established.

In *Henry v. Henry*[8] the Supreme Court stressed: "Proportionality lies at the heart of the doctrine of proprietary estoppel and permeates its every application".

Lastly one may add that the overriding principle of application of proprietary estoppel in the context of an alleged promise to make a will is that the testator is to be held to his representation only if it would be unconscionable for him to go back on it.

---

7 (2009) 3 All E.R. 945 (H.L.).

8 (2010) 1 All E.R. 988 (S.C.).

PART 2

Cyprus

CHAPTER 24

Colonial Period

The English, as earlier indicated, introduced English law in Cyprus gradually. This was in general their practice in colonies. Nonetheless, the tenor and spirit of the English law was felt from the beginning of British rule.

Procedure was the first field of legislative action. The Cyprus Courts of Justice Order in Council of 1882 marked in essence the beginning of the introduction of English law in Cyprus. Before that a High Court was established, composed of English judges, notably the High Court of Justice, in 1878.

To begin, in 1886 the Procedure Amendment Law was enacted. In the 1920's and 1930's basic aspects of English law in codified form were introduced. The English introduced, unlike England, English law in the colonies and dominions in a codified form.

In 1928 the Criminal Code in Council was introduced. In 1930 the Contract Law was enacted, notably Law 24/30, and in 1932 the Civil Wrongs Law was introduced (Law 35/32).

Ottoman Law was retained, subject to material procedural changes in its application, as the residual law of the country until 1935. In that year the Courts of Justice Order was issued, introducing English law principles in their entirety. Ottoman Law was set aside in its totality. The Criminal Procedure Law was embodied in a Code in 1949, notably CAP 14, re-enacted in 1959 as CAP 155.

In the period preceding the introduction of English law, the English judges, composing the High Court, readily had recourse to English law to avoid manifest injustice and fill gaps in the law – *Hassan v. Erikzade.*[1] At the same time they applied English rules of interpretation of the law, giving a new dimension to its application – *Aristides Ioachim v. Christofi and Christodoulo Haralambo v. Touli Haji Christofi and Another.*[2]

Gaps in the law were likewise filled by recourse to English law – *Ioannis Karageorgiades v. Christodoulo Halipariou & Sons.*[3] As to the policy of the law in general assistance was derived from English case law – *Regina v. Georghi Antoni Yallouri.*[4]

1 1 C.L.R. 84.

2 3 C.L.R. 74, 77.

3 5 C.L.R. 41.

4 3 C.L.R. 41, 44.

 | DOI 10.1163/9789004313736_025

With the enactment of the Courts of Justice Order of 1935 and the Evidence Law of the same year English law was introduced in the island in its totality subject to the following proviso: The common law and principles of equity were adopted as they stood in England in 1914. This is surprising considering that both common law and principles of equity developed subject to basic principles, flexible to the extent of meeting new needs emerging from social changes.

Possibly the intention of the legislator was to confine the principles of common law and equity to the needs of Cyprus society as they unfolded in the course of time. Be that as it may, no noticeable departure from the principles of either the common law or equity can be traced in the case law of Cyprus. In *Universal Advertising and Publishing Agency,*[5] the civil wrong deriving from false representation – passing off – although not included in the Civil Wrongs Law, found, as the court determined, application by reference to the common law. The court observed that principles of the common law in any field constitute an indivisible whole departure from which would cause great damage, breaching the harmony of the whole.

The interpretation of statutory provisions of English law followed English precedent. Characteristically, in *Georghios Milliotis v. The Commercial Firm of P. Ioannou & Co.*[6] it was held that an article of the Contract Law, incorporating a corresponding provision of English Law, should be interpreted in line with English precedent.

The Courts of Justice Order of 1935 harmonized Cyprus judicial procedure and practice with the corresponding English procedure and practice. In *Rudolf Schmuel v. The Officer in Command, Illegal Jewish Immigrants Camp Karaolos*[7] it was declared unequivocally that the means and principles that govern recourse to the court are the same as in England, including the writ of habeas corpus designed to test the legality of the detention of a person.

The principle of binding precedent applied in Cyprus in the same spirit as it did in England. Thus decisions of the High Court were binding on first instance courts. The High Court of Cyprus was bound (a) by decisions of the Privy Council before which decisions of the High Court were appealable; (b) by decisions of the Judicial Committee of the House of Lords; and (c) decisions of the English Court of Appeal and the Court of Criminal Appeal. First instance decisions of the English High Court were of persuasive, not binding, authority – *Queen v. Haralambos Erodotou.*[8]

5 19 C.L.R. 87.

6 20(2) C.L.R. 75.

7 18(2) C.L.R. 158.

8 19 C.L.R. 144, 146.

What emerges is that decisions of the High Court of Cyprus were assimilated in terms of binding precedent to first instance decisions of the High Court of England. The provisions of the 1935 Courts of Justice Order confining the application of the common law and principles of equity, as they stood in England in 1914, were ignored. There is no Cyprus precedent suggesting that principles of the common law and equity were inapplicable on the ground that they were not in existence in 1914.

The assimilation of decisions of the High Court of Cyprus to the High Court of England at first instance, was a factor restricting the adjustment of the common law and equity to the needs of Cyprus and the idiosyncracy of its people and this notwithstanding the fact that common law is a living body meant to respond to the living needs of society, as Chief Justice Hallinan underlined in *Universal Advertising and Publishing Agency v. Panayiota A. Vouros.*[9] The Chief Justice noted, inter alia, that principles of the common law of England do not fit Cyprus in their totality. He stressed that the common law must be transplanted in Cyprus as a living organism, so with the necessary legal and judicial adjustments to be in a position to meet the needs of Cyprus. At the same time he pointed out that the common law cannot flourish if partitioned by legislative definitions.

A similar approach to the identification and evaluation of the common law and its application other than in England was adopted in *Queen v. Haralambos Erodotou.*[10] So, while provocation may reduce the crime of murder to manslaughter, what constitutes provocation for the Cypriots may be different from the corresponding reaction of English people. As Lord Denning identifies in his book "Freedom under the Law", page 16 and stresses in the case of *Nyali Ltd. v Attorney-General,*[11] the principles of the common law, wise as they may be, cannot be applied with the same success outside the framework within which they were developed.

Upon a survey of the Cyprus case law it emerges, as I discern, that notwithstanding the acknowledgment that every effort must be made to adjust the application of the common law to the realities of Cyprus, little effort was made in that direction. This may be due to the fact that most judges of the High Court and all Chief Justices were English. Not until 1927 were Cypriot judges appointed to the High Court. Another reason for this lapse may be due to the absence of bodies in Cyprus entrusted to follow the evolution of the stream of the law and its direction.

---

9 19 C.L.R. 87, 94.

10 19 C.L.R. 149.

11 (1956) 1 Q.B. 16.

As a matter of principle the adjustment of the application of the common law to countries other than England must correspond to the needs of the particular country without, of course, deviation from its fundamental principles.

Notwithstanding the calamity that befell Cyprus in 1974 and the loss of a vast territory occupied by the Turkey where 70% of its productive resources lied, the Cyprus Republic sustained its integrity. So much so that she satisfied the criteria to join the European Union, which the country joined in 2004. It is worth noting the evaluation of the judiciary of Cyprus by the Committee of the European Union carried out in 2002 for the purposes of determining whether the judiciary of Cyprus satisfied the necessary criteria for joining the Union. Their assessment was the following: "The judiciary of Cyprus is independent. The principle of separation of powers is absolutely respected. The standard of justice is high".

The Constitution of Cyprus introduced in 1960 envisaged that English would be the language of the courts for the first 5 years of Independence. In 1965 this was extended indefinitely by Law 51/65. In 1989 legislation brought this to an end (Law 146/89) The writing of judicial decisions thereafter did not lessen reference to the common law and principles of equity.

CHAPTER 25

Independence

Cyprus became independent on 16th August, 1960. The Constitution provided that existing law will remain in force subject to such modifications as necessary to conform to the Constitution. Hence power was conferred upon the courts to apply preexisting law subject to such changes as necessitated by the provisions of the Constitution. The subject is addressed in Article 188.1 of the Constitution which reads:

> 1. Subject to the provisions of this Constitution and to the following provisions of this Article, all laws in force on the date of the coming into operation of this Constitution shall, until amended, whether by way of variation, addition or repeal, by any Law or communal law, as the case may be, made under this Constitution, continue in force on or after that date, and shall, as from that date be construed and applied as such modification as may be necessary to bring them into conformity with this Constitution.

Law 14/60 enacted soon after Independence provided that existing law remains in force including common law and equity. This is expressly provided by Section 29(1)(c).

The common law applied in a manner meeting the needs of Cyprus society. The principles of equity, on the other hand, are diachronically aimed at remedying shortfalls of the law within the framework of its principles, as developed in England.

The Constitution of Cyprus adopted in a distinct chapter human rights along the lines of the European Convention on Human Rights, albeit more extensively. In 1962 the European Convention on Human Rights was also adopted as part of domestic law.

The Constitution introduced two new juridical facets of great consequence: (a) Constitutionalism and (b) administrative law.

Jurisdiction for the new branches of the law was conferred upon the Constitutional Court (Articles 133–151) empowered (a) to examine the constitutionality of new laws. There was a presumption that laws enacted by the legislature were in accord with the Constitution unless declared unconstitutional by the Supreme Constitutional Court. A law declared unconstitutional lacked validity from the day of its enactment. (b) Review of the legality of

 | DOI 10.1163/9789004313736_026

actions and omissions of the executive and administrative branches of the State (article 146). It must be noted that jurisdiction to review the legality of executive and administrative acts of governmental authorities is deeply rooted in European continental law. Administrative Law as a separate branch of the law emerged in France after the French revolution as a means of testing the legality of acts and omissions of governmental authorities. A separate branch of the judiciary was established – the Council of State – vested with jurisdiction to annul illegal acts and omissions of the Government and administrative authorities. Recently administrative jurisdiction was acknowledged to the courts in England, leading to the establishment of an Administrative Division of the High Court.

After Independence decisions of the superior courts of England ceased to have a binding effect on Cyprus courts. Nonetheless, such decisions were treated as having great persuasive authority. They were often followed as a matter of course unless there was direct Cyprus authority to the contrary. In *Mouzouris and Others v Xylophagou Plantations Ltd* (1977) 2 CLR 354, it was emphasized that decisions of English Courts are of great persuasive authority, illuminating the application of common law. Likewise reference to English authority is useful in construing the legislative provisions emanating from English Law. In *Theophanous v Cosmos Insurance* (1988) 1CLR *254 at 269*, it was underlined that the principles of the common law objectively identifiable by Cyprus Courts are binding in virtue in Section 29 (1)(c) of the Courts Justice Law 14/60. The following passage from the above judgment sheds light on the approach of Cyprus Courts to the Common Law "*.... the common law is a living organism that should not be stifled by the past; its principles are intended to serve changing needs of society and should be interpreted in a diachronic perspective. Moreover, in Commonwealth countries its application should reflect the particular needs of individual societies*". (See also *Hassanein v Hellenic Island and other* (No2) (1994) 1CLR *578, 583 and Police v Xydia and Others* (1992) 2CLR *26 & David Parris v The Republic* (1999) 2CLR *186*). It must be reminded that with the exception of constitutional and administrative law, the roots of Cyprus law were English.

Common law and equity retained their importance applicable to address the needs of Cyprus society. In *Australian Consolidated Press Ltd. v. Uren*[1] the Privy Council acknowledged the right of countries where English law was in force to adjust the application of the common law to the needs of the country.

In 1964 in view of the anomalous situation that erupted in Cyprus the two superior courts were united into one, the Supreme Court of Cyprus, entrusted with the jurisdiction of the two superior courts that it replaced (Law 33/64).

1 (1967) 3 All E.R. 523.

After Independence recourse to the courts of first instance and the Supreme Court increased considerably. The constitutional entrenchment of human rights was one of the reasons for such increase.

The principle of binding precedent of decisions of the Supreme Court in its appellate jurisdiction on appeals from first instance courts and judges of the Supreme Court exercising singularly first instance jurisdiction of the Supreme Court was generally applicable. When we refer to the binding effect of decisions of the Supreme Court in its appellate jurisdiction, we mean the *ratio decidendi* of cases not obiter dicta. The Supreme Court in its appellate jurisdiction is not invariably bound by previous decisions of the court. Nevertheless they are as a rule followed in the interests of certainty of the law. There may be departure from them if this is unquestionably dictated by the commands of justice. The decisions of the Supreme Court in the exercise of original jurisdiction are only of persuasive authority. The Practice Note of the House of Lords of 1966[2] acknowledged authority to it to depart from the ratio of a previous decision when manifestly wrong. The aforesaid Practice Note was followed by the Supreme Court of Cyprus. In the *Republic (Minister of Finance and Another) v Demetriades (1977) 3 CLR 213* it was pronounced that the doctrine of judicial precedent is part and parcel of our judicial system, providing certainty in the law, equality of treatment before the law and the means for the development of legal rules in a disciplined and regular manner. (*see also Republic v Yiallourou a.o.* (*1995*) *1 CLR 363*) The decision in *Demetriades* (supra) was followed by the plenum of the Supreme Court in *Nicolaou v Nicolaou a.o.* (*No 2*) *1992 1 CLR 1330* and *Mavrogenes v The House of Representatives a.o.* (*No.3*) (*1996*) *1 CLR 315*. In both cases the Supreme Court overruled a previous decision. It is worth quoting the following passage from *Nicolaou* (supra) that was cited with approval in *Mavrogenes* (supra) at pp. 328–9:

> The boundaries and prerequisites for departure from a previous decisions of the plenum of the Supreme Court are analogous to those provided to the Judicial Committee of the House of Lords to depart from previous decisions of it, included in the Practice Note of 1966 (1966) 3 All ER 77. In the preamble of the Practice Note, adherence to precedent is reasserted as the foundation on which the law rests and its application to particular areas is determined. Only reasons of fundamental significance such as material change of circumstances on which a principle of law rests, can justify departure from the ratio of a previous decision of the Court (*Fitzleet Estates Ltd v Cherry* (*1977*) *3 All ER 998* (*HL*); *Bremer Vulkan*

2 (1966) 3 All ER 77.

> *v South India Shipping* (1981) 1 *All* ER 289; *Paal Wilson & Co v Blumental* (1983) 1 *All* ER 513; *Food Corp of India v Antclizo Shipping* (1988) 2 *All* ER 513). There is also discretion to depart from a previous decision whenever it is considered that it is based on an unquestionably wrong principle of law or leads to manifestly unjust results.

In both *Nicolaou* and *Mavrogenes* it was recognized that freedom to depart from a previous decision is unquestionably greater whenever a previous decision conflicts with constitutional principles.

The common law is applicable in all its spheres adjusted to the needs of Cyprus society. In *Katina Hadjitheodossiou v. Petros Koulia and Another*[3] it was emphasized that the common law applies as part of the law of Cyprus adjusted to meet social needs, as they emerge from time to time.[4]

The case of *KEM (Taxi) Ltd. v. Anastasis Tryphonos*[5] is indicative of the need to apply the common law in a manner responding to the needs of Cyprus society. The court pointed out that the reaction of employer and employee in the context of a labour dispute in Cyprus may take a different form from a corresponding reaction of employer and employee in England. However, on the whole Cyprus courts have been reluctant to depart from the common law as applied in England – *Antoniou and Another v. Angelides and Another.*[6]

Human rights became a significant aspect of Cyprus case law in light of their constitutional entrenchment. The spectrum of common law and equity and their principles were applied in every sphere of life subject, as indicated, to their adjustment in their application to the needs of Cypriots.

In 1974 Cyprus was struck by two catastrophic events of immense magnitude: First the coup d'etat organized and carried out by the military junta that ruled Greece that upset legality and sequentially immensely more catastrophic was the Turkish invasion that followed resulting in the occupation of 38% of the territory of Cyprus, followed by the ethnic cleansing of 80% of the Greek population of the occupied area. The ethnic cleansing of the Greeks of the occupied area was followed (a) by the movement of all Turkish inhabitants of Cyprus to the occupied area and (b) the settlement in the area under occupation of settlers from Turkey.

3 (1970) 1 C.L.R. 310. See also General Press Agency "Poulias & Konnaris Ltd. v. Christoforos Christofides, (1981) 1. C.L.R. 196.

4 See also Constantinides and Another v. Pitsillos and Another, (1980) 2 J.S.C. 279.

5 (1969) 1 C.L.R. 52.

6 (1978) 1 C.L.R. 115.

Following the collapse of the coup d'etat the courts of Cyprus condemned it in every way, supporting the supremacy of the rule of law in the country. It is important to notice that despite the ferocity of the tragic events of 1974, no state of emergency was declared. Be it noted that such power is conferred by the Constitution. The Law followed its course, reminding of the aphorism of Thomas Fuller expressed some 300 years ago that no matter how high one may stand, the law is high above him. In a decision of the District Court – Action No. 1098/75 –(unreported) the court made unqualified reference to the principle of the common law that authority to rule derives exclusively from the law.

Both the Supreme Court and District Courts condemned and decried the invasion of Cyprus by Turkey.[7]

The Turkish invasion was the greatest calamity that befell Cyprus in its long history. Resolutions of the United Nations, General Assembly and the Security Council for the withdrawal of Turkish troops from Cyprus and occupation were wholly ignored, and continue to be ignored, and the occupation continues.

Worthy of reference is the decision of the Supreme Court in *Apostolides and Others v Republic (1982) 3 CLR 928*, where reference is made to the measures taken to sustain the hypostasis of Cyprus noting at the same time "That the measures taken were not more expansive than they were, does not but reflect the desire of the people of the country not to deviate from democratic institutions, except to the extent absolutely necessary. The decision of the Supreme Court in *Alloupas v National Bank of Greece (1983) 1 CLR 55*, examines at length the doctrine of necessity and its boundaries limiting its application to what was absolutely necessary. The doctrine of necessity and range of application were recognized and defined in *Attorney General of the Republic V Imbrahim (1964) 1CLR 195*, issued on the occasion of Turkish Cypriots withdrawing from the governmental authorities and the measures necessary to sustain the efficacy of the Republic of Cyprus. As explained the doctrine of necessity has a long standing reflected in the Latin maxim *"salus populi est suprema lex"*. The aforesaid decision of the Supreme Court was treated by the Supreme Court of Canada as an unqualified reflection of the Law of Necessity in the case of *Languages Rights under the Manitoba Act 1870 (1985) 19 D.I.R. (4th) 1*. (As to the

---

7 Aristides M. Liasi & Others v. The Attorney-General and Another, (1975) 3 C.L.R. 558, The Republic v. Nicolaos Sampson, (1977) 2 C.L.R. 1, In Re Pantelis Vrakas and Another, (1977) 1 C.L.R. 70, Pavlou v. The Attorney-General, (1979) 1 J.S.C. 172, Cosma v. The Attorney-General, (1980) 1 J.S.C. 31, Righa v. The Attorney-General, (1980) 1 J.S.C. 94. See also Judgment of the Full Court of Larnaca in Civil Action 1141/75 – Vladhimiros Charalambous v. Pantelis Demetriou and Others – delivered on 17.6.1978 under appeal, Πραξικόπημα, οι Πραξικοπηματίες και το Δίκαιο – A. N. Λοίζου – Λευκωσία 1980.

law of necessity and its application in Cyprus see also "*Constitutionalism – Human Rights – Separation of Powers, The Cyprus Precedent*" by the author of the present book published by Martinus Nijhoff Publishers, Leiden / Boston, and *Kyriacou v The Republic* (1983) 3(B) 1130, *President of the Republic v The House of Representatives* (1986) 3CLR 1439 and *President of the Republic v The House of Representatives* (1991) 3 CLR 252.

CHAPTER 26

Application of Common Law after Independence

Commitment of the Cyprus judiciary to the common law and principles of equity has been unabating.

In *Constantinou v. Panayides*[1] it is clarified that the common law finds application in Cyprus in light of the provisions of Article 29(1)(c) of Law 14/60. The law attaches no qualification to the application of common law in Cyprus. As explained in the above case, what is applicable in Cyprus is the common law, not the common law as it may have been modified by English statute.

The adversarial system of justice, vital in the administration of justice, is the offspring of the common law. As explained in *Christodoulou v. Sofroniou*[2] the issues in a civil case are defined by the pleadings of either party. The duty of the litigant to put his case to the adversary through cross-examination was expounded in *Adidas v Jonitexo Ltd (1987) 1 CLR 383*, at p. 389. It was emphasised that "[l]iberty to controvert the case of the other side is at the core of the adversarial system of justice premised on the elicitation of the truth through the process of confronting the adversary with every material aspect of the party's case. In the absence of such confrontation, the Court is left with only one side of the story and may, at the end, disregard it as one sided and incompatible with the right of the opponent to be afforded a proper opportunity to put forward his case too on the subject under controversy".[3]

In *Eleftheriades and Another v. Mavrellis and Another (1985) 1 C.L.R. 436*, at pp. 444–445, the role of the judge under our adversarial system of the common law was depicted as that of an impartial arbiter; in the discharge of his adjudicative duties he must distance himself from the arena of litigation.[4] In the case of *Evangelou and Another v. Ambizas and Another (1982) 1 C.L.R. 41*, at pp. 61, 62 it was stated that:

> Although a Judge may intervene in order to ensure that the proceedings follow the course ordained by the rules of evidence and procedure, he must avoid interfering beyond the limits indicated above and especially refrain from passing unnecessary comments that may create the

1 (1984) 1 C.L.R. 466 (C.A.).
2 (1987) 1 C.L.R. 441 (C.A.).
3 See also Vasos Taki v The Rerpublic (2009) 2 CLR 599; Pal a.o. v The Republic (2010) 2 CLR 551.
4 See also Eleftheriades v Cyprus Hotels (1985) 1 CLR 677.

 | DOI 10.1163/9789004313736_027

> impression of his descending into the arena of trial. A Judge must invariably distance himself from the conflict that unfolds before him and maintain strictly his arbitral position throughout the proceedings.

In *Pastella Marine v. Iranian Tanker*[5] it is underlined that in asserting the principles and range of application of the common law guidance may be derived from English case law.

In Sekavin S.A. v. Ship "PlatonCh".[6] it is reminded that Section 70 of the Contract Law, Cap. 149. reproduces the common law principle of quasi contractual liability. In Saab and Another v Holy Monastery of Ayios Neophytos (1982) 1 CLR 499, it was propounded that Section 73 of Cap. 149, "aims to reproduce the common law rules on damages for breach of contract, as they crystallized and were fashioned in the case of Hadley v. Baxendale [1843–60] All E.R. Rep. 461. (See Marcou v. Michael, 19 C.L.R. 282)".[7] Amongst other aspects of contract law in which English case law has been followed are those relating to rescission of contract[8] (Section 63); undue influence[9] (Section 16); misrepresentation[10] (Section 18).

In *Ioannou v. Kounnides*[11] it was decided that the relevant principles of the common law referable to trusts are not ruled out by the provisions of Section 106 of the Contract Law, Cap. 149.

In Kakoullou and Another v Kakoulli (1985) 1 CLR 335, it was stated that "the Civil Wrongs Law is a codification of the English Common Law and should be interpreted and applied in accordance with the principles of the Common law of England". In *HadjiTheodossiou v. Koulia and Another (1970) 1 C.L.R. 310*, it was stated that Section 51 of the Civil Wrongs Law, Cap. 148, purports to codify the English Common Law regarding the tort of negligence. English precedent on the tort of negligence[12] was followed and applied in a number of instances

---

5 (1987) 1 C.L.R. 583 (F.B.).

6 (1987) 1 C.L.R. 297 (Single Judge).

7 See also Aristodemou v Charalambous (1990) 1 CLR 319; Charalambous a.o. v Liberty Life Insurance (2011) 1 CLR 1739.

8 See Cyprus Agriculture and Transport Co Ltd a.o. v The Attorney General (1971) 1 CLR 267; "Savvides Christofides" v Christofidou (1978) 1 CLR 303; Stavrou v Demetriou (1991) 1 CLR 304; A.N. Stasis Estates Ltd v George Evans Edwards a.o. (1995) 1 CLR 385.

9 See Patsalidou v Kyriakides (1979) 1 CLR 71; Ioannou v Charalambidou (1988) 1 CLR 555; Socratous v Sivitanidi (1998) 1602.

10 See Georgiou a.o. v Alpha Concrete Ltd (2009) 1 CLR 1049; Mountis v Maxdata Holdings Ltd (2012) 1 CLR 2367.

11 (1998) 1 C.L.R. 1215.

12 See Cyprus Wine Association Ltd v Goerghiou (1970) 1 CLR 246; A-G V Pentaliotis & Another (1998) 1 CLR 1931.

including, inter alia, the duty of occupiers towards invitees;[13] the duty of a master towards his employees to secure a safe system of work;[14] the duty of medical practitioners to their patients;[15] the duty of architects[16] and of lawyers[17] owed to their clients; negligent misrepresentation causing economic loss.[18]

The principle of duty of care expounded under English law is also applied in relation to negligent driving under Section 8 of the Motor Vehicles and Road Traffic Law of 1972 (Law No 86/72).[19]

In *Christodoulou v Menicou (1966) 1 CLR 17* it was observed that with regard to contributory negligence, Section 57 of our Civil Wrongs Law, Cap. 148, reproduces the provisions of the English Law Reform (Contributory Negligence) Act, 1945, thus rendering English case law directly relevant. This was reaffirmed in *Cyprus Palestine Plantations Co Ltd v Leandrou (1982) 1 CLR 880.* The issue of contributory negligence often arises in road collision cases.[20] *In Adidas v Jonitexo Ltd (1987) 1 CLR 383,* it was decided that the tort of passing off is codified in Cyprus by Section 35 of the Civil Wrongs Law; the codification is not exhaustive but may be supplemented by the principles relating to the tort as known in English law.[21]

The principles on which compensation is awarded to dependents in fatal accident cases are based on English case law,[22] as well as the principles governing the award of damages for pain and suffering in personal injury cases.[23]

The law of defamation governed by Sections 17–25 of the Civil Wrongs Law is another area in which English precedent was followed in conjunction with the right to freedom of speech guaranteed by article 19 of the Constitution of Cyprus and article 10 of the European Convention on Human Rights.[24]

---

13 G.I.P.Construction Ltd V Neophytou a.o. (1983) 1CLR 669.

14 Cyprus Palestine Plantations Co Ltd v Leandrou (1982) 1 CLR 880.

15 See Athanasiou v Kounounis (1997) 1CLR 614; Angeli Christos v Vorka (2007) 1 CLR 761.

16 See Lappas v Pafitis (1995) 1CLR 832.

17 See Beaumont a.o. v Papacleovoulou (2010) 1 CLR 525.

18 See Premier Chemical v The Bank of Cyprus Ltd (1998) 1 CLR 1951.

19 See inter alia Murrel v The Police (1994) 2 CLR 217; Silvestrou v The Police (1996) 2 CLR 151; Kyriakou a.o. v Kanari (1997) 1 CLR 1436.

20 See Charalambous v Kassapis (1988) 1CLR 25.

21 See also Hadjikyriakos Co v United Biscuits (1979) 1 CLR 689.

22 See Kazakou v Avraamide (2000) 1 CLR 1626; E.A.C. v Kyriakou a.o. (2006) 1 CLR 417; Niki Demetriou a.o. v Hadjisavva a.o. (2009) 1 CLR 848.

23 See Paraskevaides (Overseas) Ltd v Christofi (182) 1 CLR 789; Mavropetri v Louca (1995) 1 CLR 66.

24 See, inter alia, Alithia Publishing Company a.o. v Alonefti (2002) 1 CLR 1863; Loucaides v Alithia Publishing Company (2003) 1 CLR 22; Arktinos Publications v Doros Georgiades (2011) 1 CLR 407; Drousiotis v Papadopoulos (2012) 102.

English precedent has also been followed in interpreting the relevant provisions of Cap 148, governing the liability of joint tortfeasors[25] (Section 11); liability for acts of an independent contractor[26] (Section 12); vicarious liability[27] (Section 13); the torts of detinue and conversion[28] (Sections 37–39); trespass to immovable (Section 43)[29] and movable property (Section 44); public nuisance[30] (Section 45) and private nuisance[31] (Section 46), interference with easement of light (Section 50);[32]damage caused by dangerous things – the rule in Ryland v Fletcher[33] (Section 52).

The common law principles were also followed with regard to the award of exemplary damages for civil wrongs.[34]

The defence of estoppel per rem judicatam in civil proceedings is another aspect of the English common law applied in Cyprus.[35]

In *Paikkos v. Kontemeniotis*[36] it is recalled that the common law finds application where no reference is made to a principle of the common law in the statute on a subject. Hence it was decided that the right conferred by the common law to take action for malicious prosecution is applicable notwithstanding absence of reference to it in the criminal law statute. The common law was applicable in all its length. This is made clear in *Constantinou v Panagides (1984) 1CLR 466*, where it was decided that enticement of the wife, actionable of common law, is equally applicable in Cyprus.

---

25 Mouhurem v Pavlides (1983) 1 CLR 526.

26 Zivlas v Municipality of Limassol and Another (1979) 7 J.S.C. 989; Gavriel & Another v Electricity Authority (1980) 1 CLR 55.

27 Hellenic Mining Co Ltd v Galaxy Tours Ltd (1978) 1 CLR 414; Demosthenous v Katsourides (1988) 1 CLR 665; Potamitis a.o. v Ioannou (1992) 1 CLR 479; Brodie a.o. v Theodorou a.o. (1998) 1 CLR 1632; Municipal Corporation of Limassol v Constantinou (1972) 1 CLR 119; Costa v Municipal Corporation of Limassol (1975) 1 CLR 84; Tsiopanis v Avraam (1978) 1 CLR 27; Makris v Petrou (1984) 1 CLR 362.

28 Panayi v Artemiou & Others (1976) 3 J.S.C.510.

29 See Kakoullou and Another v Kakoulli (supra); P & A Enterprises v Louis Tourist (1987) 1 CLR 142.

30 See Sofocleous & Another v Georghiou & Another (1978) 1 CLR 149.

31 See Palantzi v Agrotis (1968) 1 CLR 448; Araouzos and Another v Ioannou (1980) 1 CLR 591; Hadjichristodoulou v Aristedou (1981) 1 CLR 297.

32 See Akama and Anther v Tsiakoli (1967) 1 CLR 206.

33 E.A.C. v Kannava (2000) 1 CLR 425.

34 See Papakokkinou and Others v Kanther (1982) 1 CLR 65; Kennedy Hotels Ltd v Indjirdjan (1992) 1 CLR 400; Erotokritou v Theodorou and Another (1997) 1 CLR 1800; Papakokkinou a.o. v Municipality of Paphos (1998) 1 CLR 634; Mita v G.K Sophocleus (2003) 1 CLR 1952.

35 Theori a.o. v Djoni a.o. (1984) 1 CLR 298; Gavriel and Another v Agapiou v Another (1998) 1 CLR 1868; Pamporides v Κτηματική Τράπεζα Κυπρου (1995) CLR 670.

36 (1989) 1 C.L.R. 50 (C.A.).

Of consequence is the decision in *Demades Overseas Ltd. v. Studio M.A. St. Ltd.*[37] where it was held that if the codification of the common law is not complete, recourse can be had to the common law for further guidance. A similar approach was followed in Ioannou v. Kounnides.[38]

The decision of doubtful correctness is *Kyriakides v. Aristidou*[39] where it was decided that the Civil Wrongs Law, Cap. 148 embodies the jurisprudence of the courts up to the date of its enactment.

In *Azinas and Another v. Police*[40] there are also passages that are hard to reconcile with the current of the common law. It was said, inter alia, that it is safer to approach a case having in mind the provisions of the Criminal Code rather than turning to the English common law which does not constitute directly the prototype of our legislation. This, to my mind, is wrong. The common law, as earlier stated, is part of the legislation of Cyprus and recourse may be had to it if the code – in this case the Criminal Code – that embodies English law, does not include a provision of it.

In *Riverside Navigation v. Hambury& Co.*,[41] following the decision in *Asimenos and Markou v. Chrysostomou and Another*,[42] the court held that Rule 237 of the Admiralty Jurisdiction Order 1893 makes applicable in all cases not provided for by the aforementioned order English rules that were in force on the day immediately preceding the Independence of Cyprus.

Under the common law a right to appeal a first instance decision was bestowed only by the legislature.

In *Republic v. Ermogenous & Others*[43] the court noticed that under the common law the right to appeal emanates exclusively from statutory law.

The decision of *The Republic v. Zypiti*[44] is indicative of the impact of the Constitution upon the applicability of principles of the common law. Article 172 of the Constitution provides:-

> The Republic shall be liable for any wrongful act or omission causing damage committed in the exercise or purported exercise of the duties of officers or authorities of the Republic. A Law shall regulate such liability.

37 (1996) 1 C.L.R. 799 (C.A.).
38 Civil Appeals 9795 – 96 – 98 1C – J.S.C. 1215.
39 (2000) 1 CLR 349.
40 (1981) 2 C.L.R. 1 (C.A.).
41 (1988) 1 C.L.R. 195 (Single Judge).
42 (1982) 1 C.L.R. 145 (C.A.).
43 (1990) 2 C.L.R. 459 (C.A.).
44 (2003) 1(b) C.L.R. 749 (C.A.).

The court held that the provisions of the above Article of the Constitution superseded the provisions of the common law definitive of the obligation of state authorities to keep the roads in a good state. A detailed examination of Article 172 is to be found in the subsequent case of *Georghiou v The Attorney – General (1982) 1 CLR 938*. It was held that section 28 of the Civil Wrongs Law, limiting liability of a master or principal for assaults of his servants to cases of express authorisation or subsequent ratification "does not aim to regulate liability under Article 172 for injurious unjust acts of the officers of the Republic committed in the exercise or purported exercise of their duties. In short it has no relevance to the liability of the State for acts of its servants. If s.28 is at all relevant, it comes in conflict with Article 172 to the extent that it limits the liability of the Republic for certain manifestly wrongful acts contrary to the very letter of the aforesaid article of the Constitution. If s.28 was held to be reconcilable with the Constitution, it would open the door to the State, limiting its liability for a variety of wrongful acts, neutralizing thereby the mandatory provisions of the Constitution that make no distinction between the wrongful acts in the sense of Article 172 for which the State may be held liable". The said decision was followed in *Pitsillos v The Republic (1984) 1 CLR 780*.

An important aspect of the common law refers to the respect owed to the judicial process. Such respect is material for the fruition of justice. Abuse of the process of the court and its consequences are adopted in Cyprus along the lines of English Law. In *Constantinides v Vima Ltd (1983) 1 CLR 348,* following English precedent on abuse of process, it was held that the exercise by the appellant of his statutory right of appeal, while questioning the impartiality of the judiciary through the press amounts to a gross abuse of the process of the Court; and that, therefore, unless the appellant first restores the authority of the Court, it would be an abuse on his part to invoke its powers to obtain justice in the case. Had this grave abuse of process not been restrained, the floodgates of abuse of the process of the Court by trial through the press would be opened to the detriment of the Judiciary. In the decision it was emphasised that "The Supreme Court has inherent power not only to restrain abuse of process but also to secure obedience to the law – *Hammersmith v. Magnum Automated Forecourts [1978] 1 All E.R. 401 (CA)*. Its power may be exercised whenever the justice of the case so requires – *AG v. Chaudry [1971] 3 All E.R. 946 (CA)*". The decision in Constantinides (supra) was followed by the plenum of the Supreme Court in *Director of Prisons v Jennaro Perrela (1995) 1 CLR 217 and Constantinides v Komodromou* (supra). In the latter decision extensive reference is made to English case law on abuse of process. It was decided (by majority) that the parallel commencement of a civil suit and a private criminal prosecution by the same litigant for a bounced cheque, did not amount to an abuse of process since each of the two proceedings serves a different purpose in law.

In *Korellis v. Attorney-General*[45] it was decided that the Assize Court has no inherent jurisdiction to order the prosecuting authority to disclose evidential material founding its case to the defence before trial, in the absence of express statutory provision. In *Gigas v Ousta (No.1) (1994) 1 CLR 109*, it was held that the Supreme Court has inherent jurisdiction to reinstate an appeal only in instances where refusal to reinstate would be tantamount to deprivation of a right guaranteed under Article 30.3(b) of the Constitution.[46]

The right of every citizen to prosecute, known as a private prosecution, vests in every citizen injured by a criminal act, intonating that there is nothing in the Constitution neutralizing the position at common law as regards a private prosecution –*Tofinis v. Theocharides.*[47] The position in *Tofinis* was followed in *Kalia v. Lambrou,*[48] confirming that when proprietary rights of an individual are directly encroached upon by structures erected in contravention of the Streets and Buildings Law (Cap. 96) the individual has a right to institute a criminal prosecution in respect of the contravention.(see also *EPIA Ltd V Sirocco Estates Co Ltd a.o. (1997) 2CLR 424, Charalambides v Komodromou 2002 2CLR 518 and Demosthenous v Typhonos – issued on 16.1.2013 Criminal Appeal No 153 / 2011 (not yet reported).*

It is interesting to cite an extract from the judgment of one of the two majority judges, whose decision marked the outcome of the appeal in *Savva "Pambos" v. The Police,*[49] *delineating the application of English law in the field of criminal procedure in Cyprus*:

> Although our code of Criminal Procedure – Cap. 155 – derives from English law and is modeled on the common law adversarial system of criminal justice it reflects, as often the case with codified legislation, the complexion of English law on the subject at the time of its codification. Our code of Criminal Procedure was not specifically codified for Cyprus but represents a model of criminal procedure introduced by the British in their former colonies, a model that broadly reflects English procedure and practice in criminal cases(1). Notwithstanding codification, English

45 (1998) 1 C.L.R. 1718 (C.A.).

46 See also A.N. Stasis Estates Co Ltd v Ioannou (2000) 1 CLR 1082.

47 (1983) 2 C.L.R. 363 (C.A.).

48 (1985) 2 C.L.R. 217 (C.A.).

49 (1986) 2 C.L.R. 30 (C.A.).

practice and procedure are still relevant in two respects: First, as a supplement to the code "as regards matters of criminal procedure for which there is no special provision in this law" as stated in s. 3, Cap. 155. Second, as an aid to the interpretation of the provisions of Cap. 155 that have their counterpart in English law. English cases on the interpretation of English law are particularly helpful as a guide to the interpretation of similar or comparable provisions in our statute. Further to the above, English practice and procedures are always relevant to the extent that they illuminate the fundamental precepts of criminal justice under the common law.

The English law and rules of evidence are rendered applicable in Cyprus by virtue of section 3 of the Evidence Law, Cap. 9, save as otherwise provided in the said law. Some notable examples of the application of English law are the principles relating to the standard and burden of proof;[50] corroborating evidence;[51] the dangers of convicting on the uncorroborated evidence of an accomplice;[52] witness with an interest to serve;[53] circumstantial evidence;[54] similar fact evidence;[55] identification;[56] refreshing of memory;[57] mixed statements;[58] the rule against the admission of hearsay evidence[59] and its exceptions (abolished by Law 32(I)/2004).

---

50 See Charitonos a.o. v The Republic (1971) 2 CLR 40; Loizou v The Police (1989) 2 CLR 363; Paphitis v The Police (1990) 2 CLR (102; Soteriades v The Police (1991) 2 CLR 482; Pengeros v The Republic (1995) 2 CLR 143; Xydas v The Republic (2012) 2 CLR 807.

51 See Ttooulias v The Police (1989) 2 CLR 2 258; Michaelidou v The Police (1989) 2 CLR 172; Parmaxis v The Republic (1997) 2 CLR 224.

52 See Tooulias v The Police (supra); Aeroporos a.o. v The Republic (1993) 2 CLR 362; Yiouroukis v The Republic (1993) 2 CLR 231; Kafkaros a.o. v The Republic (1995) 2 CLR 51; Christodoulou alias Ropas a.o. v The Republic (No.2) (2000) 2 CLR 628; Petrosyan v The Republic (2003) 2 CLR 90.

53 See Mousoulides v The Republic (1983) 2 CLR 336; Papachrysostomou v The Police (1988) 2 CLR 55.

54 See Fournides v Republic (1986) 2 CLR 73; Michaelides v The Republic (1989) 2 CLR 172; Paphitis v The Republic (supra) ; Xydias a.o. v The Police (1993) 2 CLR 174; Psomas v The Republic (1993) 2 CLR 312.

55 See inter alia Nikolaou & Sons Ltd v District Labour Officer (1991) 2 CLR 261.

56 See Sophocleous v The Republic (1998) 2 CLR 259; Hadjigeorgiou v The Republic (1995) 2 CLR 174; Neophytou v The Police, Criminal Appeal No 127/2011, judgement dated 12.03.2013 (unreported).

57 See Koufou v The Republic (1984) 2 CLR 165.

58 See Konstantinou v The Police (1989) 2 CLR 109.

59 See Vasiliades v The Police (1988) 2 CLR 193; Police v Xydia & Another (1992) 2 CLR 26.

Lastly prerogative writs notably habeas corpus, a mantle of freedom under the common law, mandamus, prohibition, quo warranto and certiorari were given constitutional protection by Article 155 of the constitution. No leave of Court is required for invoking habeas corpus to check the legality of the detention of an individual. For the remaining prerogative writs leave to apply is required upon establishing a prima facie case.[60] It must be explained that prerogative writs have no application in the domain of administrative law governed exclusively by Article 146 of the Constitution. The English rules of procedures applicable before independence continue to find application after independence.

60 In re Kakos 1885 1 C.L.R. 250; In Re Aeroporos 1988 1 C.L.R. 302; In re Anthimou 1991 1CLR 41; In re Hadjisavva 1993 1 C.L.R. 102; In re Kalfopoulou 1998 1 C.L.R. 55.

CHAPTER 27

Cyprus Case Law on the Applicability of the Principles of Equity after Independence

The powers of trustees and personal representatives and the powers of the court for the appointment of trustees are regulated by the Trustee Law, Cap. 193. Below reference will be made to a number of Cyprus decisions reflecting the application of the principles of equity in Cyprus very much along the lines of their application in England.

In *National Bank of Greece v. Masonou*[1] the court declared that equity intervenes to stop abuse of a legal right in an effort to moderate the rigour of contract law. Further, the court stressed that equity stepped in to fill the gap and close the door to a party's insistence on his/her contractual rights in circumstances that would lead to manifest injustice.

In *Iranian Tanker v. Pastella*[2] the court clarified that equity applies in Cyprus as part of domestic law in virtue of the provisions of Section 29(1)(c) of Law 14/60.

In *Demetriou a.o. v. Xandri*[3] it was decided that there is no right to invoke the principles of equity in the absence of the necessary factual background. As earlier noted, the decisions of Cyprus courts after 1989 were written in Greek. Hence the title of the cases is translated and referred to in English.

In accordance with Cyprus case law the equitable doctrine of promissory estoppel applies in Cyprus in much the same way as it does in England.

In *Limmare Shipping v. Boustani*[4] the court held that the doctrine of promissory estoppel applies where a person by his words or conduct makes another person to a transaction a promise or gives an assurance which is intended to affect the legal relations between them, and the other party acts upon it altering his position to his detriment; the party making the promise or assurance will not be permitted to act inconsistently with it.[5]

---

1 (1980) 1 C.L.R. 195 (C.A.).

2 (1987) 1 C.L.R. 120 (Single Judge).

3 (2012) 1 C.L.R. 2184 (C.A.).

4 (1981) 1 C.L.R. 386 – Savvides.

5 See also Hadjiyiannis v. Attorney-General of the Republic, (1970) 1 C.L.R. 32, 38–39.

 | DOI 10.1163/9789004313736_028

In *Stylianou v. Papacleovoulou*[6] the court acknowledged that proprietary estoppel also applies in Cyprus in much the same way as it does in England, adding that in appropriate circumstances estoppel may arise from silence. Estoppel also operates at the early stage of judicial proceedings, entitling a person in possession of immovable property to retain possession pending trial. The standard of proof at an early stage of the proceedings , i.e. interim order, is "probability of success". The said decision was followed in *Odysseos v. Pieris Estates and Others.*[7] In *Odysseos* (*supra*) it was observed that by virtue of sections 4 of Cap. 224 of the Immovable property (Tenure, Registration and Valuation) Law Cap. 224, as amended, "[t]he existence of a constructive trust cannot in Cyprus create an estate in Land, unless there is compliance with the provisions for the Sale of Land (Specific Performance) Law, Ca. 232 as amended. Consequently a contract for the sale of land cannot be enforced either by the purchaser or an assignee in the absence of strict compliance with the provisions of Cap. 232". It was clarified (p. 571) in *Papacleovoulou* (supra) that "the relation between the person asserting property rights and the registered owners was not that of purchaser and vendor. The registered owners were bare trustees having done all in their powers to divest ownership of the property and pass it on to the person from whom the plaintiffs had acquired the land. That they did not accomplish their intention was due to a mistake liable to be rectified".

In *Miltiadous v Miltiadous (1982) 1 CLR 797*, the contribution of the wife to the acquisition of the matrimonial house was held to give rise to the creation of a resulting, implied or constructive trust, following the decision of the House of Lords in *Gissing v Gissing (1970) 1 All ER 780*, and subsequent authorities affirming the same principle. The Supreme Court stated in its judgment that under English law "[t]he existence of a trust has been implied whenever spouses or couples in co-habitation made a joint contribution to the setting up of a house for common use. .... A trust is deemed to arise upon the coincidence of two things: (a) the pooling of resources and/ or the exertion of efforts for the acquisition of immovable property, provided the contribution made by each individual is substantial; (b) the existence of such a relationship as to justify the attribution of a common intention to enjoy the use of the property together". The aforesaid decision was followed in *Theodoulou v Theodoulou (1987)*

6 (1982) 1 C.L.R. 542 (C.A.).

7 (1982) 1 C.L.R. 557 (C.A.); see also Christoforou V Christoforou in Relation to Resulting or Constructive Trust (1998) 1 CLR 1551 and Papakokkinou a.o. V Municipality of Paphos (1998) 1 CLR 2398.

1 CLR 1010; *Pentafkas v Pentafka* (1991) 1 CLR 547; and *Stylianou v Stylianou* (1999) 1 CLR 1833.

In *Orphanides v Orphanide* (1998) 1 CLR 179, it was held that by virtue of Section 14 of the Regulation of the Property Relations of the Marital Couple Law of 1991, Law 232/91, governing the right to property in the event of dissolution or annulment of the marriage or in case of dissolution of the marital relationship, the equitable principles of English law do no longer apply in this field. Section 14 is a definitive provision regulating the division of property rights of a disunited marital couple.

In *Markidou v. Kiliaris*[8] it was held that as far as the transfer of property is concerned, the assignee is in no better position than the assignor. Further the court decided that the prayer for estoppel was inconsistent in the particular case, notably a claim by an assignee against the owner of property claiming damages for breach of contract.

The concept of ownership under Section 1(1)(a) of the English Administration of Justice Act of 1956, applicable in Cyprus, is not limited to legal ownership but extends to "beneficial" or "equitable" ownership as well – *Papadopoulos & Others v. Blue Emblem.*[9]

Specific performance is an equitable remedy. Equity does not act in vain. On the other hand, there is ample authority that no decree of specific performance can be issued where the agreed term has expired or will expire before a decree can be made.[10]

In *Christofides v. Kotzianastase*[11] the court adhering to previous authorities affirmed that the principles of equity are applicable unless there is a different regulation on the subject by statutory law. It was further acknowledged that the principles of the common law were complemented by the principles of equity, conferring, inter alia, power upon the courts to order specific performance.

The grant of equitable relief extends to many areas of judicial proceedings. As underlined in *Iranian Tanker v. Pastella,* the principles of equity are part of the law of Cyprus, incorporated by the provisions of Section 29(1)(c) of Law 14/60.

In *Mouchtou and Others v. Himarou*[12] it was repeated that the principles of equity are applicable in the absence of specific provision in the legislation regulating a subject. Of course, no recourse can be made to the principles

---

8 (1983) 1 C.L.R. 392 (C.A.).

9 (1985) 1 C.L.R. 453 (Single Judge).

10 See Paraskevas v Alpan (Taki Bros) 1 CLR 224.

11 (1993) 1 C.L.R. 718 (C.A.).

12 (2001) 1C C.L.R. 1794.

of equity in the absence of the necessary substratum. No recourse to the principles of equity can be made in the absence of the necessary factual background. – *Demetriou and Others v. Xandri.*[13]

There is no rule either of equity or the common law imposing an obligation on the plaintiff to aid a tortfeasor to lift the wrong done to the plaintiff –*Gavri and Others v. Pashiou.*[14]

13 (2012) 1 C.L.R. 2184.

14 (2004) 1(A) C.L.R. 125.

CHAPTER 28

Epilogue

Reviewing the impact of the common law on British civilization one can be led to the following conclusions:

(a) It led to peaceful co-existence in communities of people in the early period of Anglo-Saxon settlements in England.
(b) Gradually it was extended with considerable effect to the rights of citizens, aspects of which assumed the significance of constitutional rights.
(c) The courts identified the common law and the rights conferred thereby on citizens, giving written expression to them. Their contribution to the development and extension of the common law to meet new needs of society cannot be overestimated.
(d) The co-existence of the common law with statutory law was harmonious.
(e) Claims by the Crown to stand above the Law were rejected by the courts with determination, law being declared as the supreme authority. The rule of law took the upper hand gaining the characterization of sovereign law.
(f) Equity played a dominant role in the ascent of natural justice as a binding legal principle.
(g) The attachment of legal status to the application of equity reinforced the conformity of the law with pananthropic justice – "Reason stripped of human passion".
(h) The English judiciary played a very significant role in the incorporation of equity in the system of justice, strengthening the commitment of people to the rule of law. One can only hope that the penetration of equity into the law will be further strengthened. Justice should be the guide in the formation of the law.

Effect of the Common Law and Principles of Equity on British Society

The common law and thereafter the principles of equity had a beneficial influence on English society. The system developed was conducive to the liberty of the subject, opening the horizon for the use of the creative powers of man in all fields of philosophy, science, technology and the arts.

It is no coincidence that the industrial revolution first occurred in England.

 | DOI 10.1163/9789004313736_029

Introduction of English Law in Cyprus

English law, common law and equity being its founding premises, was passed on to British colonies and dominions, being the greatest legacy left by the British. In other respects colonial rule was dominated by imperialism.

The inheritance of English law in Cyprus had positive effects in relation to human rights, including property rights. It is no coincidence that despite the blows inflicted upon Cyprus in 1974, the rule of law retained its force, the State survived, helping in the sustenance of the Republic of Cyprus becoming in due course a member of the European Union. The introduction of a comprehensive code of human rights in the Constitution was another consequential factor giving universal character to law, entrenching its premises. I may conclude by saying that human rights generate the creative powers of mankind.

Summary

Preface

England

Chapter 1 – pp. 3–8: Genesis of the Common Law

Emergence of the common law
Process of development of the common law
Systematization of the common law
Philosophy of the English legal system
Supremacy of the law
Bills of Rights 1629 and 1689
Judicial precedent
Application of the common law not static – flexible to the extent of meeting new needs of society

Chapter 2 – pp. 9–12: Introduction to the Common Law

Common law and statutory law became the principal sources of English law
Equity – a complementary source of law evolved in the interests of justice
Equity – Pananthropic law – Magna Carta of 1215 – England a colonial power
Transmission of English law to British colonies, including Cyprus and dominions
Retention of English law in Cyprus after Independence
English law was gradually introduced in colonies

Chapter 3 – pp. 13–18: Application and Development of the Common Law

Common law developed gradually and steadily
Reference to judicial decisions instantiating the application of the common law in England
Development of the common law through the case law
The commitment to the rights of a person was unabating
The rights of a person at common law must be in compliance with natural justice

Judges can expand the common law by applying it to new situations by reference to its core principles, not by evolving legal principles of their choice

It is desirable that the common law should develop in countries of the Commonwealth homogenously, subject to the special needs of each country

Common law is not extinguishable by statute unless this is made clear by the statute or by clear indication

The rules of litigation evolved under the common law are inapplicable to administrative inquiries

The judiciary made a significant contribution to the development of the common law

At common law an open system of justice is the rule

Procedural fairness is an aspect of the common law

Chapter 4 – pp. 19–20: Binding Precedent

Binding precedent – A fundamental rule of the English administration of justice

Object of binding precedent

Certainty about the law

Binding precedent closely associated with the hierarchy of the judiciary

Decisions of higher courts are binding on decisions of lower courts

Decisions of House of Lords, succeeded by the Supreme Court, are binding on the Court of Appeal and courts below

The Supreme Court and the Court of Appeal may deviate from previous decisions of their own in rare circumstances where principles of previous decisions are regarded as manifestly wrong

Decisions of the High Court are of persuasive authority on the court itself but binding on lower courts

Reference to a number of decisions illustrating the application of binding precedent

Chapter 5 – pp. 21–26: Basic Principles of the Common Law

Common law recognized a number of fundamental human rights

The development of the common law in various countries of its application should, as a rule, be homogenous

Common law recognized constitutional rights

Freedom of the press was recognized at common law as a matter of particular importance

Common law rights of a person should be in conformity with natural justice

Fundamental rights recognized by common law were not as extended as modern charters and conventions on human rights

Common law developed to meet changing circumstances and patterns of society to which it is applied

The right to join a union was recognized at common law as a fundamental right

Gradually the application of the common law by the courts was often referred to as judge made law

Common law develops incrementally and logically

Chapter 6 – pp. 27–30: The Amdinistration of Justice

Natural justice is at the root of the common law rules relevant to the administration of justice

Reference to a number of decisions explanatory of procedural fairness in the administration of justice

Speedy determination of trials was a fundamental rule of the administration of justice, a principle incorporated in Magna Carta – Justice delayed is justice denied

Detailed reference to judicial decisions exemplifying fundamental rules of the administration of justice

It must be noted that courts have no jurisdiction to abolish common law crimes

Chapter 7 – pp. 31–34: Supplementary Reference to Principles of the Common Law

Extensive reference to decided cases shading light on the application of the principles of the common law

Reference to some decisions exemplifying the application of the common law. The categories of public interest are not closed.

At common law the sheriff was liable for illegal and offensive acts of his officers

The sources of the common law in the absence of judicial decisions are:

(a) opinion of textbook writers; (b) judicial dicta and reports of Commissions and Legal Committees; (c) analogies with legal systems that share the common law heritage

The power of a police constable, at common law, to arrest a person to avert breach of the peace.

The right to life acknowledged by the European Convention on Human Rights had no counterpart at common law

Oral evidence regarded as the best evidence

Common law right to be heard by an administrative authority before taking a decision likely to adversely affect a person

Establishments qualifying as charities

Principles of open justice could be developed by the courts as a matter of common law

Chapter 8 – pp. 35–38: Overview of the Common Law

Common law, the offspring of the Anglo-Saxon communities who settled in England in the 5th century CE

The conquest of England by the Normans in 1066 left unaffected the development of the common law

Common law principles had a twofold purpose: (a) to sustain human rights and (b) to ensure orderly life in the communities where people resided

Courts played a dominant role in the identification of the principles and rules of the common law and its development to meet new needs emerging from the evolution of society and advances in the field of technology

English judges never assumed the role of law makers

The legislature never abrogated or sought to abolish or play down the existence of the common law

England never had a written constitution

The adoption of codes and conventions on human rights after the end of the 2nd World War enriched English law

The expansion of the common law to meet changing social circumstances was repeatedly proclaimed as part of the constitutional role of the courts.

Chapter 9 – pp. 39–42: Origin and Principles of Equity

Equity incorporates pananthropic law

Equity is meant to fill gaps in the law enabling the court to do what is right in the interests of justice

Equity is akin to natural law

Equitable rights and defences operate only on the conscience of the plaintiff

Equity treats as done that which ought to have been done

Reference to a number of cases illustrating the application of equity

Equity retains its flexibility to meet unforeseen circumstances in the past

Equitable damages is the means to compensate a person for non pecuniary loss

Although equity will not help a volunteer, it will not strive officially to defeat a gift

The twelve maxims of equity

Equity does not interfere to grant relief in commercial agreements

Where a party to a contract acts extortionately, oppressively or coercively towards the other party, the court in fairness will set aside the transaction

Equitable rights and defences operate only on the conscience of the plaintiff

Courts apply principles of equity expansively, treating equity as the embodiment of universal rules of justice

Dishonesty in equity entails (a) dishonest conduct by the standards of reasonable and honest people and (b) awareness that by these standards the conduct of a person is dishonest

Equity rendered a transaction tainted by mistake voidable

Chapter 10 – p. 43–44: Instantiation of the Application of the Principles of Equity

Legal precedent does not curtail the stream of equity, having at its core conscience

Hereafter in the following chapters reference will be made to the application of the principles of equity in various domains of life

Chapter 11 – pp. 45–46: Breach of Confidence

Breach of confidence justifies equitable protection and relief

An injunction is the appropriate remedy of stopping the passing off of confidential information

A solicitor stands in a confidential relationship to a person to whom he/she renders legal advice

Identification of the principles relevant to breach of confidence in cases other than contract: (a) the information must have the quality of confidence'

(b) it was received in circumstances importing an obligation of confidence and (c) unauthorized use of it to the detriment of the party communicating it.

An agreement set aside for breach of confidence entitles the plaintiff in equity to damages

Wife standing as surety to her husband

Equity protects the wife from liabilities or obligations undertaken who acts as surety to her husband under inordinate pressure from her husband

The case law signifies the cases under which a wife may be relieved from the guarantee of obligations of her husband

Chapter 12 – p. 47–48: Undue Influence

Undue influence may be exerted by husband upon his wife

Circumstances under which she may be entitled to relief examined

A party seeking relief from a transaction on grounds of undue influence must show: (a) that the transaction was manifestly disadvantageous for him and (b) restitution in respect of all that the party gained from the exercise of undue influence

Detailed examination of the principles governing obligations undertaken by a wife as surety of her husband to a bank

Chapter 13 – pp. 49–50: Cause of Action and Issue Estoppel

Finality of litigation is definitive about the parties' rights and obligations

Cause of action estoppel is a principle of equity

Issue estoppel arises in relation to issues raised in an action, including issues that could have in logic been raised in the proceedings

In equity the court is entitled to make an order for disclosure of information by a non-party to the proceedings

Chapter 14 – p. 51–52: Trusts

Reference to the definition of the word "trust" and "trusts"

A trustee in the exercise of his duty can only take into consideration relevant considerations to the trust

A liquidator stands in the position of a trustee

In human exchanges a trust may arise in circumstances warranting the interposition of equity

Constructive trusts

Chapter 15 – p. 53–54: Duress

Duress in equity is assimilated to fraud or undue influence

The doctrine of duress and the doctrine of equitable estoppel arising from undue influence have much in common

Release from obligations given by "A" to "B" will in equity be ineffective if the releasee dishonestly withheld facts bearing on the release

Chapter 16 – p. 55–56: Specific Performance

Specific performance is an equitable remedy empowering the court to order the execution of a contract, provided the subject matter of it is identifiable as in the case of land

Equity also acknowledges partial performance as a legitimate remedy

Chapter 17 – p. 57–58: Set Off

Whenever appropriate and so warranted by justice, the court may take into consideration a counterclaim by the defendant

There is a right of set off in equity of an unliquidated claim for damages

Generally a demand for unliquidated damages can give rise to an equitable set off

Set off may be allowed where it would be manifestly unjust to allow the plaintiff to enforce payment without taking into account the cross claim

Chapter 18 – p. 59–60: Equitable Assignment

Equity recognizes the assignment of rights to property – movable or immovable

The assignee retains in equity a right over the subject of assignment

The assignee becomes in equity the owner and controller of a legal chose and is entitled to sue for the recovery of it

As a matter of practice the court requires him to join the assignor as plaintiff or, if he/she refuses, to join the assignor as defendant

Laches can only bar equitable relief, not a statutory right

Equitable damages is the means to compensate non pecuniary damage

Chapter 19 – p. 61–62: Laches

The defence of laches must be founded on equitable principles

Chapter 20 – p. 63–64: Subrogation

Subrogation does not rest on contract

It is a principle of equity to avoid injustice

No subrogation arises between insurance companies

Chapter 21 – pp. 65–66: Estoppel

The Concise Oxford Dictionary defines both words "estop" and "estoppel" – Definitions incorporated

Estoppel is a principle of equity as affirmed in judicial decisions

As a rule estoppel arises whenever a representee has relied on a misrepresentation, thereby altering his position, by going ahead with a transaction

There is a presumption that a representee acted on a promise made

The representation, as the case law establishes, must be unequivocal

The sufferance of detriment by the representee, although a corollary in most cases of a misrepresentation, is not an invariable prerequisite for founding equitable estoppel

Prerequisites for establishing estoppel: (a) clear representation that the representor will not insist on the enforcement of strict legal rights and (b) in the circumstances it would be inequitable not to allow the representee who has been so influenced by the representation as to warrant the intervention of equity

Estoppel by representation is a rule of evidence justifying in appropriate circumstances the stoppage of the representor from averring facts contrary to his representation

Estoppel may arise from words or conduct

Estoppel is a private law concept

As the case law demonstrates, there has been considerable expansion of estoppel in recent years

Estoppel plays a dominant part in mitigating the rigours of strict application of the law

Decisions contrary to natural justice are void but, until so declared by a court of law, they are heeded by the law

Chapter 22 – p. 67–68: Promissory Estoppel

Promissory estoppel renders a promisor bound by his promise notwithstanding the absence of legal obligation

Whenever the representation of a party is intended to be binding and intended to be acted upon, equity will impose estoppel

Chapter 23 – pp. 69–70: Proprietary Estoppel

Proprietary estoppel aims to confer rights to property arising from a promise

The object, as in the case of promissory estoppel, is to hold a person bound by his representation, including representations regarding the conferment of property

Prerequisites of proprietary estoppel defined: (a) there must be acquiescence or encouragement and (b) proprietary estoppel is not dependent on awareness by the parties of their rights and consequential readiness by the representor to compromise them

Proprietary estoppel is limited to proprietary rights in land

The overriding principle of proprietary estoppel is that a party must be held to his representation if it would be unconscionable to do otherwise

Proportionality lies at the heart of the doctrine of proprietary estoppel and permeates its every application

Cyprus

Chapter 24 – pp. 73–76: Colonial Period

Cyprus came under British occupation in 1878 after a defensive agreement with Turkey that retained sovereignty over the island. In 1914, when England and Turkey found themselves on opposite sides in the first world war,

England denounced the agreement of 1878 and declared Cyprus to be a British colony.

During British occupation English law was introduced in Cyprus gradually – firstly in the area of the administration of justice and sequentially in every field of law, including common law and equity. The introduction of English law in its totality was completed in 1935.

The High Court was at first composed exclusively of English judges who often made reference to aspects of English law before 1935.

The 1935 Courts of Justice Order made specific reference to the introduction of common law and equity as they stood in England in 1914. The case law of Cyprus proved that this was of no significance. Cyprus courts followed the common law and principles of equity as they were shaped by English judicial precedent.

Cypriot judges were appointed to the Supreme Court for the first time in 1927.

The 1974 disaster afflicted Cyprus as a result of the coup d'etat staged by the Greek military junta that governed Greece and sequentially the catastrophic Turkish invasion and occupation of 38% of the Cyprus territory resulting in the ethnic cleansing of 80% of the population of the area, notably Greek Cypriots. Notwithstanding the calamity of 1974, the Cyprus Republic sustained its hypostasis as a living state, becoming in 2004 a member of the European Union.

Chapter 25 – pp. 77–82: Independence

Cyprus became independent on 16th August, 1960. The written Constitution of the island provided that existing English law would continue to apply subject to such modifications as necessary to bring it into conformity with the Constitution. Sequentially a law was enacted in 1960 (14/60), making the existing English law applicable, including the common law and principles of equity.

The Constitution of Cyprus incorporated human rights in a very comprehensive way.

After Independence decisions of superior courts of England ceased to be binding but were often referred to and treated as of persuasive authority.

The anomalous situation that prevailed in 1964 led to the union of the two superior courts, notably the Supreme Constitutional Court and the High Court, vesting their jurisdiction to the Supreme Court of Cyprus.

The principle of binding precedent of decisions of the Supreme Court was retained as in England.

Reference to Cyprus case law illuminating the application of common law in Cyprus.

Chapter 26 – pp. 83–92: Application of Common Law after Independence

Commitment of the Cyprus judiciary to the common law and principles of equity

Reference to a number of judicial decisions demonstrating the application of the common law during colonial rule

Chapter 27 – pp. 93–96: Cyprus Case Law on the Applicability of the Principles of Equity after Independence

Reference to a number of decisions of the Supreme Court of Cyprus instantiating the application of equity

Equity intervenes to stop abuse of a legal right in an effort to moderate the rigour of contract law

The necessary factual background essential for the application of equity

Promissory and proprietary estoppel find full application

Specific performance is an equitable remedy

Equity applies unless there is a different regulation on the subject by statutory law

Chapter 28 – pp. 97–98: Epilogue

(a) Impact of the common law on British civilization;
(b) Role of equity in the ascent of natural justice;
(c) Effect of the common law and principles of equity on British society'
(d) Introduction of English law in Cyprus

www.ingramcontent.com/pod-product-compliance
Lightning Source LLC
Chambersburg PA
CBHW031327230926
51848CB00001B/131